Med

The Ultimate Guide to
Cooking and Eating Mediterranean

TABLE OF CONTENTS

MEDITARRANEAN RECPIES

INTRODUCTION

There is no denying that the Mediterranean is a beautiful part of the world. Tourists from all over the globe visit the area to admire the architecture, the natural landscape, and historical landmarks. It is easy for visitors to adopt the active lifestyle and the laid back attitudes that the Mediterranean is known for.

It's also easy to see why Mediterranean cuisine is lusted over and enjoyed by all who indulge. The culinary delights that originate in Southern Europe, Northern Africa, Italy, Spain and parts of the Middle East are well known and highly sort after. The foods that are produced in these areas are certainly varied, but there is one thing they all have in common; and that is that the cuisine is attractive and flavourful, with a multitude of health benefits.

Fortunately, you don't need to book an airline ticket or a cruise ship to enjoy what Mediterranean cuisine has to offer. In addition to being to incredibly good for your health, you can achieve the look and taste of Mediterranean cuisine to enjoy in your own home.

REGIONS OF MEDITERRANEAN CUISINE

There are lots of elements that can make food distinctly Mediterranean. For the most part, it's the location. Parts of the world that share the shores of the Mediterranean sea are where the cuisine originates and can be divided into three main areas: Southern Europe, North Africa, and Eastern Mediterranean.

Countries in the South of Europe such as Spain, Italy and the southern regions of France use many ingredients that are prominently found in Mediterranean cuisine. Unlike Northern Africa and Eastern Mediterranean countries, wine is a very important component of the southern European dining experience. Wine is used in cooking, but also to share at the table among friends.

Northern Africa is characterized by its use of spices to create flavorsome dishes. Areas such as Algeria, Tunisia, and Morocco use plenty of saffron, coriander, cumin, cloves and paprika to create robust aromas and depth of flavor. Fruits and nuts are also commonly used in these areas within stews and curries. The sweetness from apricots and raisins are commonly used to balance out the heat from fiery Harissa, as well as preserved lemons, which are used to add the salty element.

Eastern Mediterranean can be defined by the traditional flavors found in Greece and Turkey. It also incorporates Middle Eastern cuisines from Syria, Palestine, Lebanon, Egypt, and Israel. Fresh cheeses such as Feta and Haloumi feature heavily, as well as many sauces and condiments made from yogurt. Parsley, mint, and lemons lead the way to flavor many spreads and dips.

All of these regions combine to make up what is commonly known as the Mediterranean. With so many varied cultures and history within these countries, it's little wonder there is such variety across Mediterranean cuisine. Variety in spices, flavors, grains, meats and seafood ensures there really is something to suit everyone's tastes.

Concerns   Areas   Good + Evil
Bishop   Allen   Clyde
|
|
Hosp. follow up
704 - 348 - 2950
Kayla C. Whisenhunt
Brijjit

704- 731-6934- nepology
980-
Todd Isshe

ESSENTIAL INGREDIENTS FOR MEDITERRANEAN COOKING

There are many ingredients that are essential to Mediterranean cooking. If you are new to this cuisine, it can be a little overwhelming. With this list, you can begin to stock the essential items that are used regularly in Mediterranean cooking.

SPICES

Bay Leaves: This is the aromatic leaf of the Bay tree. Bay leaves are rich in Vitamin A & C, potassium, calcium and magnesium. Bay leaves have also been proven effective in the treatment of migraines. Store dried bay leaves in an airtight container in your pantry.

Cardamom: You can purchase Cardamom as a ground spice or as in pod form. This spice is made from the seeds of several plants and it's great for boosting digestive health and relieving mild stomach pain.

Ground Coriander: This spice is made from the ground seeds of the coriander plant (also known as Cilantro.) Ground coriander is great for your digestive health and liver function.

Ground Cumin: Ground cumin is made from the seeds of a flowering plant that grows native in the Middle East all the way to India. Ground Cumin is known to have anti-inflammatory properties and is also a rich source of iron.

Dried Thyme: This is the dehydrated and dried version of the fresh and aromatic Thyme plant. Thyme is high in antioxidants and can improve circulation.

Turmeric: Turmeric has long been used throughout India and is the spice that gives any dish a vibrant yellow color. Turmeric has been linked to improved brain function and has anti-inflammatory properties.

Dried Oregano: Oregano is derived from a flowering plant that belongs to the Mint family. It is native to the Mediterranean region and has long been used for its medicinal properties for treating infections and as a natural insect repellent.

Saffron: These thin red strands are amongst the most expensive spices on the market. Saffron has a rich, distinctive flavor. It has been known to improve mood and act as an aphrodisiac.

PANTRY ITEMS

Couscous: Often mistaken for a grain, couscous is actually pasta that is made from semolina flour. Couscous contains antioxidants and is known to reduce the likelihood of chronic disease.

Bulgur Wheat: Bulgur is most often made from Durum wheat and is particularly popular in Middle Eastern dishes. This ancient whole grain is packed with fiber, protein, and vitamins.

Lentils: These are legumes that are small and round in shape. You can purchase in cans that are ready for immediate use after being rinsed. Dried lentils may need to be soaked in water overnight to soften. Lentils are high in fiber and folate and can help to reduce cholesterol levels.

Canned Beans: Kidney and Fava beans, as well as chickpeas, are great ingredients to have on hand in your pantry. They store well, are inexpensive and very good for you. Chickpeas, in particular, are a great source of protein, vitamin K and zinc.

Canned Tomatoes: Diced tomatoes or whole peeled tomatoes feature heavily in Mediterranean cooking. They are relatively inexpensive and great for adding to soups and stews. Tomatoes promote good stomach health and have been known to reduce blood pressure.

Balsamic Vinegar: Balsamic is a very dark and intensely flavored vinegar that originated in Italy. It has many uses in the kitchen, from salad dressings and marinades to vinaigrettes and sauces. Balsamic has been known to improve one's skin tone and promote weight loss.

Olives: Black and green olives stored in jars in your pantry will be incredibly convenient when cooking Mediterranean cuisine. Olives are small stones fruits that have a salty flavor and are associated with cardiovascular health.

Olive Oil: This oil is made from pressing whole olives. There are a wide variety of olive oils on the market and it can be confusing as to which is best. As a general rule of thumb, extra-virgin olive oil should be used predominantly for dressings, dips and drizzling. By the best quality extra-virgin olive oil that you can afford for this purpose. For sautéing and frying, it is not as important to have high-quality olive oil, as a lot of the flavor is lost through the heating process.

Pasta: Pasta is made from flour mixed with either water or eggs and sometimes both. Originating in Italy, dried pasta is a convenient and versatile pantry staple for Mediterranean cooking. Small shapes can be added to soups and stews, where are larger and longer pasta shapes tossed with herbs and a delicious sauce are a meal within itself.

Rice: Wild rice, brown rice, basmati rice, and jasmine rice, so many to choose from! Rice is a great foundation for many Mediterranean dishes included Middle Eastern curries or Spanish Paella. Having a variety of different rice varieties in your pantry will ensure you have the perfect accompaniment to your delicious meal.

CHEESES

Feta: This cheese originated in Greece and is made from sheep's milk, goat's milk or a combination of both. It is crumbly in texture and salty in flavor. Feta is incredibly versatile and can be crumbled on top of pizza, a frittata, and salad or eaten with antipasto. Feta is a source of protein, good fats, and calcium.

Mozzarella: Mozzarella is a firm white cheese that originated in Italy. It pairs beautifully with tomato and basil, and it's commonly found atop a pizza or ripped into salads. Mozzarella is also coveted for it melting capabilities and is a great source of good fats and calcium.

Goats Cheese: As the name suggests, this cheese is made from goat's milk and has a distinctive earthy flavor. Cheese made from goat's milk is lower in lactose than those made with cow's milk, and it's a good source of vitamin B3 and calcium.

THE MEDITERRANEAN DIET

Health professionals and nutritionists alike have identified the benefits of a diet rich in Mediterranean cuisine. It is also easy to adhere to given that there is so much variety in the dishes that look and taste fantastic.

The Mediterranean Diet focuses on:

Plant-Based Foods: Food in the Mediterranean is predominantly plant-based. Fruits are eaten as breakfast and for dessert. Stews, curries, and soups are full of vegetables, beans and legumes. Seeds, nuts and spices are used for their flavor and for their health benefits. Bread, grains pasta and rice provide the foundations for many Mediterranean dishes.

Eating seasonally: Consuming the fruits and vegetables that are in season has two main benefits. Fruits and vegetables that are in season often have a fuller flavor and higher nutritional content. When vegetables and fruits are in season they are generally more competitively priced. You can research your local area to understand what produce is in season and when is the best time to utilize them.

Unprocessed Food: The Mediterranean diet uses little to no processed foods. This enables you to avoid the nasty preservatives and chemicals that can come with pre-packaged 'convenience' foods. Keep your shopping simple by purchasing meat, seafood, vegetable, and fruits. Apart from some canned items such as beans, tomatoes, and legumes, there should be little need for processed items in the Mediterranean diet.

Dietary Fat: Olive oil is used as the main source of dietary fat on the Mediterranean diet. Other food sources such as avocados and nuts will provide healthy fats to your diet, although olive oil will be the main source.

Eggs: The Mediterranean diet uses a small number of eggs, and suggests that eggs are limited to approx. five per week.

Dairy: Cheese, yogurt and other dairy foods should be consumed in moderation. Often in Mediterranean cuisine yogurt is used as a condiment and should not impact your consumption too much. Cheese such as feta and goat's cheese are generally crumbled sparingly onto a salad of frittata, meaning you can still enjoy the delicious flavors these products provide without overindulging.

Poultry, Seafood and Red Meat: The Mediterranean diet uses a wide variety of protein sources that are derived from meat and animal products. The key here is to keep the meat portions small. The meat component of your meal should only be a third, with the remainder of your meal being plant-based foods.

Alcohol: Wine consumption is limited to one glass per day for women and two glasses per day for men. Enjoy wine with your main meal if you desire.

The Mediterranean diet appeals to a wide variety of people regardless of age, gender and fitness levels. Nutritionists and health professionals recommend the Mediterranean diet as a way of eating and enjoying the things you love in moderation. The Mediterranean diet does not impose harsh restrictions. It does not follow strict regimes and rules.

The food you consume should be in line with the values of the Mediterranean, enjoying fresh and flavorsome food, enjoying everything in moderation and enjoying your life.

Breakfast

Get your morning off to a great start with this selection of Mediterranean inspired breakfast dishes. If your mornings leave you little time to prepare a nutritious breakfast, look for the options that can be frozen and reheated, or made in batches to store in the fridge.

Gingerbread Quinoa Bake With Banana

Greek Yoghurt Pancakes

Mediterranean Breakfast Sandwich

Honey Almond Ricotta with Peaches

Mediterranean Breakfast Salad

Greek Omelette Casserole

Baked Eggs in Tomatoes

Quinoa Breakfast Skillet

Baked Eggs with Avocado and Courgette Noodles

Honey Caramelized Figs with Yoghurt

Greek Eggs with Quinoa

Mediterranean Style Scrambled Eggs

Vegetarian

One of the main concepts of the Mediterranean diet is that our plates are loaded with vegetables. If you normally eat a lot of red meat or poultry, take a little break with these delicious vegetarian options.

Mediterranean Stuffed Peppers

Mediterranean Slices

Grilled Vegetable & Feta Tart

Mediterranean Fig & Mozzarella Salad

Mediterranean Feta Salad With Pomegranate Dressing

Mediterranean Potato Salad

Orzo & Mozzarella Salad

Roasted Aubergine With Bulgur & Zesty Dressing

Crispy Greek-Style Pie

Vegetarian Casserole

Potato Frittata With Pesto & Goat's Cheese

Minted Courgette Salad

Soup

Soup is the ultimate comfort food. Piping hot bowls of luscious soups make even the coldest winters bearable. Make a large pot and freeze in portions to have on hand for a quick dinner or lunch.

Yellow Gazpacho

Quick Chickpea, Tomato, And Pasta Soup

Lentil And Spinach Soup With Pomegranate Molasses

Mediterranean Fish Stew

Italian Sausage Minestrone

Green Chili Chicken And Bean Soup

Moroccan Chickpea & Lentil Soup

Mediterranean Quinoa Soup

Kale, Cannellini And Farro Stew

Mediterranean Tomato Soup

Greek Chickpea Soup With Lemon

Mediterranean Potato Soup

Roasted Tomato & Mascarpone Soup

Chunky Mediterranean Vegetable Soup

Seafood

You don't have to live close to the Mediterranean Sea to enjoy great seafood. Fish, shrimp, lobster, and scallops are great sources of protein are low in fat. Combined with the traditional flavors of the Mediterranean and you'll create a dish that tastes great, and is great for you.

Spicy Shrimp With Cauliflower and Arugula

Baked Ginger Salmon in Parchment

Greek Shrimp Farro Bowls

Mediterranean Couscous with Tuna and Pepperoncini

Mediterranean Cod

Roasted Mediterranean Shrimp With Quinoa

Sautéed Shrimp & Fennel

Shrimp Pasta With Whole-Wheat Spaghetti

Grilled Salmon With Mediterranean Salsa

Mediterranean Fish Packets

Grilled Tuna With Olive Relish

Seafood Ceviche

Mediterranean Roasted Mackerel

Mediterranean Penne With Anchovies & Tomatoes

Mediterranean Cod

Mediterranean Stuffed Swordfish

Sardine And Olive Tart

Bucatini Alla Puttanesca

Mediterranean Seared Scallops

Greek Baked Scallops Santorini

Chicken and Poultry

Chicken is incredibly versatile meat, which carries Mediterranean flavor very well. It can be roasted, grilled, shredded, served warm or cold making chicken an adaptable protein with a variety of uses.

Chicken with Sun-Dried Tomatoes and Artichokes

Greek Chicken with Pasta

Lemon Chicken Risotto

Fennel Chicken Puttanesca

Spiced Pan-Roasted Chicken with Olives, Figs, and Mint

Easy Lemon Chicken Asparagus

Cilantro Lime Chicken with Avocado Salsa

Honey-Lime Chicken Parcels

One-Pot Greek Oregano Chicken and Orzo

Chicken with Courgettes

Italian Turkey Meatballs

Whole Roasted Rosemary Spatchcock

Red Meats

*Beef and Lamb are consumed infrequently in the Mediterranean.
However, when lamb or beef in on the menu, is it always succulent,
juicy and tender. Larger cuts are slow roasted or braised and always
packed with flavour.*

Garlic and Anchovy Roasted Lamb chops

Moroccan Goat Curry

Mediterranean Lamb Bowls

Middle Eastern Meatballs in Saffron Curry sauce

Mediterranean Beef Stew

Grilled Beef Shawarma

Spanish Paprika Beef

Italian Beef Ragout

Mediterranean Lamb Pizza

Lamb Roast with Lemon and White Wine

Mediterranean Meatloaf

Veal Campagnola

Veal Scaloppini With Spicy Tomato And Caper Sauce

Mediterranean Stuffed Pork Cutlets

Spicy Lemon Garlic Pork

Mediterranean Lamb and Vegetable Couscous

Breakfast Dishes

GINGERBREAD QUINOA BAKE WITH BANANA

PREP: 10 MINS   **COOK:** 80 MINS   **SERVES:** 4

This modern take on porridge uses Quinoa instead of oats. Perfect for a winter morning.

INGREDIENTS

3 cups mashed banana, approx. 3 large bananas

¼ cup molasses

¼ cup Maple Syrup

1 tablespoon ground cinnamon

2 teaspoons vanilla extract

1 teaspoon ground ginger

1 teaspoon ground cloves

½ teaspoon ground allspice

½ teaspoon salt

1 cup quinoa, uncooked

2 ½ cups almond milk, unsweetened

¼ cup slivered almonds

METHOD

1. In a large casserole dish, stir together the banana, molasses, maple syrup, cinnamon, vanilla extract, ginger, cloves, allspice and salt. Mix well to combine. Add the quinoa and stir well until the quinoa is incorporated.

2. Add in the almond milk and mix until well combined. Cover and refrigerate overnight.

3. In the morning, heat your oven to 350 degrees. Give your mixture a quick whisk to ensure the quinoa hasn't settled on the bottom.

4. Cover the pan tightly with foil and bake until the almond milk is absorbed, and the top of the quinoa is set. It should take between an hour and 1 hour and 15 mins.

5. Remove the foil and sprinkle the cinnamon and slivered almonds on top and allow to stand for 10 minutes before serving.

GREEK YOGHURT PANCAKES

PREP: 15 MINS   **COOK:** 15 MINS   **SERVES:** 4

Fluffy light pancakes served with fruit? Yes, please!

INGREDIENTS

1 ¼ cup plain flour

3 tablespoons butter unsalted, melted

3 eggs

1 ½ cups plain Greek yogurt

½ cup milk

¼ teaspoon salt

2 teaspoons baking powder

1 teaspoon baking soda

¼ cup of sugar

1 cup fresh seasonal fruit to serve

METHOD

1. In a large bowl, Whisk the flour, salt, baking powder, and baking soda together in a large mixing bowl.

2. In a separate bowl, whisk together the melted butter, eggs, milk, yogurt, and sugar. Mix until you achieve a smooth consistency.

3. Pour the yogurt mixture in the mixing bowl with the dry ingredients. Stir well to combine. Allow the pancake batter to sit for 10-15 minutes.

4. Heat a large non-stick frying pan or pancake griddle over medium heat. Cook the pancakes in batches, spooning approx. a ¼ at a time for each pancake. When the bubbles burst, flip with a spatula to cook the other side. Pancakes should be golden brown in color.

5. Serve the pancakes immediately with a scoop of Greek yogurt and fresh seasonal fruit like berries, figs or bananas. A drizzle of honey is delicious too.

MEDITERRANEAN BREAKFAST SANDWICH

PREP: 5 MINS   **COOK:** 5 MINS   **SERVES:** 1

Wrap it up and take this sandwich on the go to keep your morning moving.

INGREDIENTS

1 teaspoon butter

¼ cup egg whites whisked (approx. 2 egg whites)

1 teaspoon chopped fresh herbs such as parsley or basil

1 whole grain bread roll

1 tablespoon basil pesto

1 slice cheese (Provolone or Cheddar work great)

½ cup semi-dried tomatoes

METHOD

1. Heat a small frying pan over medium heat and melt the butter. Pour in the egg whites and season well with salt and pepper.

2. Sprinkle with fresh herbs. Cook for approx. 3 minutes or until the egg is set, flipping once with a spatula.

3. While your egg is cooking, toast your roll under a grill or in a toaster. Spread the roll with pesto.

4. Assemble your sandwich by stacking the cooked egg, cheese, and semi-dried tomatoes, and place the bread roll half on top.

HONEY AND ALMOND RICOTTA

PREP: 3 MINS   **COOK:** 3 MINS   **SERVES:** 1

This Ricotta spread could have many uses and is very versatile. Serve on bagel or toast for a quick breakfast, or spoon onto pancakes for a delicious treat. Serve the Ricotta with fresh seasonal fruit and a drizzle of honey for a simple dessert.

INGREDIENTS

1 cup whole milk ricotta

½ cup sliced almonds

¼ teaspoon almond extract

1 teaspoon honey

Zest from 1 orange or lemon

METHOD

1. Combine ricotta, almonds and almond extract in a medium sized mixing bowl and gently stir to combine. Transfer to a serving bowl and sprinkle with additional sliced almonds and drizzle with a teaspoon of honey.

Ricotta is fantastic for spreading and dolloping in many ways. Use your imagination to flavor your ricotta to your taste. Savory combinations such as tomato and basil, as well as dill, served with smoked salmon would work really well.

MEDITERRANEAN BREAKFAST SALAD

PREP: 10 MINS   **COOK:** 10 MINS   **SERVES:** 4

Salad might not be the first thing that comes to mind as a breakfast dish, but why not? Give it a try. It might surprise you!

INGREDIENTS

10 cups mixed salad leaves

2 cups cherry tomatoes, halves

4 eggs

½ cucumber, chopped into bite-sized chunks

1 cup cooked quinoa, cooled

1 large avocado, peeled and diced

1-cup nuts chopped – use cashews, almonds or walnuts

½ cup mixed herbs like basil, parsley, dill or oregano

Extra virgin olive oil

One Lemon

METHOD

1. Bring a saucepan of water to boil. Using a spoon lower the eggs into the boiling water and reduce to a simmer. Cook eggs to your liking, for soft-boiled, approx. 6 minutes. Peel and set aside.

2. Combine the salad leaves, tomatoes, cucumber and quinoa in a large mixing bowl. Drizzle with olive oil, season well with salt and pepper and toss well to combine.

3. To serve, portion out the salad between four plates and top with sliced avocado. Top with an egg (halved) and sprinkle with herbs and a squeeze of lemon. Add more seasoning to the eggs if required and drizzle with olive oil. Serve immediately.

GREEK OMELETTE CASSEROLE

PREP: 15 MINS   **COOK:** 40 MINS   **SERVES:** 12 Slices

*If you've got a big crowd to feed at breakfast time, this Greek
Omelette Casserole could be the answer. Alternatively, cut into
slices and store in airtight containers in the fridge for up to four days.*

INGREDIENTS

12 large eggs

2 cups whole milk

100g fresh spinach

2 cloves garlic, minced

300g jar artichokes (with olives and peppers) drained

and chopped

150g jar sun-dried tomato feta cheese, crumbled

1 tablespoon fresh chopped dill (1 teaspoon dried dill)

1 teaspoon dried oregano

1 teaspoon lemon pepper

4 teaspoons olive oil, divided

METHOD

1. Heat oven to 375F/180C fan/gas 6. Prepare the fresh herbs and artichoke, olives, and tomatoes by chopping finely.

2. Heat a large fry pan over medium heat and add 1 tablespoon of olive oil. Sauté the garlic and spinach until wilted.

3. Grease a baking dish (9" x 13") and layer the spinach/garlic and the artichoke, olives, and tomatoes evenly over the base of the dish.

4. In a large mixing bowl, whisk the 12 eggs together with the milk, fresh herbs, and lemon pepper. Season well with salt.

5. Pour the egg mixture into the baking dish and sprinkle over the crumbled feta.

6. Bake in the oven for 40 minutes or until set.

BAKED EGGS IN TOMATOES

PREP: 10 MINS   **COOK:** 10 MINS   **SERVES:** 4

This breakfast is a real showstopper. It looks impressive, but it's super simple to make.

INGREDIENTS

2 tablespoons olive oil

8 medium tomatoes

8 large eggs

¼ cup milk

¼ cup Feta cheese crumbled

4 tablespoons chopped fresh herbs (Italian parsley and/or basil work well)

METHOD

1. Heat oven to 375F/180C fan/gas 6. Using a small sharp knife cut a 1" hole around the tomato stalk. Use a spoon to scoop out the seeds and juice from inside the tomato. Repeat with the remaining seven tomatoes. *Save the tomato juice and seeds for making salsa at a later date.

2. Place the tomatoes into a muffin tray with the cut hole side facing up; the muffin shape will help to keep the tomatoes upright during the cooking process. Crack one egg into each tomato and season with salt and pepper.

3. Put 1 tablespoon of milk, and 1 tablespoon of Parmesan on top of each egg.

4. Bake for approx. 15 minutes or until the eggs are set to your liking and the tomatoes have softened a little.

5. Top with a sprinkling of fresh herbs and serve immediately.

QUINOA BREAKFAST SKILLET

PREP: 10 MINS   **COOK:** 10 MINS   **SERVES:** 4

You can totally customize this to your taste. Remove the bacon for a vegetarian option if you like, and substitute the vegetables for what you have on hand.

INGREDIENTS

4 slices thick-cut bacon, chopped

1 small eggplant, chopped into small chunks

½ red onion, diced finely

½ red pepper, diced finely

½ green pepper, diced finely

1 cup sliced mushrooms, chopped

2 garlic cloves, crushed

½ cup uncooked quinoa, rinsed

1 cup vegetable or chicken stock or water

4 eggs, cooked to your liking

METHOD:

1. Heat a large skillet over medium heat. Sauté the diced bacon until the fat has rendered away and the bacon is crispy. Remove from the pan and drain well on kitchen paper.

2. Add the peppers, onion, eggplant, garlic to the pan and cook for 5-6 minutes, stirring occasionally until the vegetables soften.

3. Add the uncooked quinoa and stir to combine with the vegetables and lightly toast for 2 minutes.

4. Pour the stock (or water) into the pan and bring up to the boil. Season well with salt and pepper. Turn the heat down to low and cover. Simmer for 15 minutes until the liquid is absorbed and the vegetables are tender.

5. While the vegetables and quinoa are cooking, you can prepare your eggs how you prefer them.

6. To serve, spoon the quinoa mixture into bowls and top with an egg. Serve immediately.

BAKED EGGS WITH AVOCADO AND COURGETTE NOODLES

PREP: 10 MINS   **COOK:** 10 MINS   **SERVES:** 4

Add some courgettes to your breakfast for a morning veggie boost.

INGREDIENTS

3 courgettes, spiralized into noodles

2 tablespoons extra-virgin olive oil

4 large eggs

Pinch of Paprika for garnishing

Fresh basil, for garnishing

2 avocados, halved and thinly sliced

METHOD

1. Preheat oven to 350F/180C. Prepare a baking tray with baking paper, or lightly spray with olive oil.

2. Combine the courgette noodles and the olive oil in a large mixing bowl. Divide into four portions on your baking tray. Shape the noodled into a bowl/nest shape.

3. Crack an egg into the center of each courgette nest and place the baking tray into the preheated oven. Bake until the eggs are set, approx. 10 minutes.

4. Season the eggs well with salt and pepper and sprinkle with a little paprika. Serve with avocado slices.

HONEY CARAMELIZED FIGS WITH YOGHURT

PREP: 10 MINS **COOK:** 10 MINS **SERVES:** 4

A light summery breakfast with a little sweetness is bound to get you moving in the mornings!

INGREDIENTS

2 cups low fat plain Greek yogurt

Pinch of ground cinnamon

8 fresh figs, halved

1 tablespoon of honey, plus a little extra to drizzle

¼ cup chopped pistachio nuts

METHOD

1. Heat the tablespoon of honey in a pan over low/medium heat. Place the figs in the pan, cut side down until caramelized, approx. 5 minutes.

2. Spoon the Greek yogurt into bowls and top with the warm figs.

3. Sprinkle the pistachios and cinnamon on top and drizzle with honey to serve.

GREEK EGGS WITH QUINOA

PREP: 10 MINS   **COOK:** 20 MINS   **SERVES:** 6

The mornings can be a busy time. Get a head start by making a large batch of Greek Eggs. Store in an airtight container and enjoy all week long!

INGREDIENTS

12 eggs

¼ cup plain Greek yogurt

1 teaspoon onion powder

1 teaspoon garlic powder

½ teaspoon salt

½ teaspoon pepper

1 teaspoon olive oil

150g bag baby spinach

250g cherry tomatoes halved

1 cup feta cheese

2 cups cooked quinoa

METHOD

1. Start by whisking your eggs together in a large mixing bowl, season well with salt and pepper. Add the garlic powder, onion powder, and Greek yogurt and whisk all together until well combined.

2. Heat the olive oil in a large frying pan over medium heat. Add the spinach and toss until it starts to wilt.

3. Add the cherry tomatoes and cook for 3 minutes until soft.

4. Pour the egg mixture into the pan and cook until set, about 7 to 9 minutes. Stir continuously as they cook so the eggs are scrambled.

5. Once the eggs are almost set, stir through the Feta and the cooked quinoa until well combined and heated through.

MEDITERRANEAN STYLE SCRAMBLED EGGS

PREP: 5 MINS   **COOK:** 5 MINS   **SERVES:** 2

Looking for a quick no-fuss breakfast? Have this on the table in 10 minutes flat.

INGREDIENTS

1 tablespoon olive oil

3 eggs

1 tomato, roughly diced

1 cup baby spinach leaves

2 tablespoons feta cheese, crumbled

2 slices of wholegrain bread to serve, toasted

METHOD

1. Lightly whisk the three eggs in a small bowl with a fork. Season well with salt and pepper and set aside.

2. Lightly sauté the tomato for 2 minutes, then add the baby spinach and toss till wilted.

3. Pour the egg mixture into the pan and stir slowly with a spatula, scraping the egg mixture from the bottom of the pan as it begins to set. This will only take about 2 minutes.

4. Serve your scrambled eggs on a toasted whole grain bread slice and sprinkle with crumbled feta.

Vegetarian Dishes

MEDITERRANEAN STUFFED PEPPERS

PREP: 15 MINS   **COOK:** 25 MINS   **SERVES:** 2

These stuffed peppers will make a divine light lunch or a perfect side dish.

INGREDIENTS

1 large red and 1 large yellow bell pepper (capsicum) halved

with seeds removed. Leave stalk attached for presentation.

85g Couscous

50g feta cheese, crumbled

50g semi-dried tomatoes

25g pine nuts, toasted

A small handful of black olives, roughly chopped

A handful of cherry tomatoes cut in quarters

2 tablespoons fresh basil, shredded

METHOD

1. Heat oven to 200C/180C fan/gas 6. Heat the peppers on a plate in the microwave for 5 mins to soften them a little. Place on a lined baking tray with the cut side up.

2. Place the couscous in a bowl and cover with 125ml boiling water. Stir to combine the water and couscous. Cover the bowl and leave to stand for 10 mins. Using a fork, fluff the couscous to break up any lumps. Mix in the basil, feta, pine nuts, olives, and tomatoes. Spoon the couscous mixture into the pepper halves. Bake in the oven for 10 mins.

MEDITERRANEAN SLICES

PREP: 10 MINS   **COOK:** 20 MINS   **SERVES** 4

Keeping a stock of sliced roasted peppers, artichokes and puff pastry in your freezer and you'll never be stuck for a quick brunch or elegant appetizer.

INGREDIENTS

4 tablespoons green (basil) pesto

375g puff pastry, ready rolled

140g sliced roasted peppers, frozen

140g frozen artichokes (about 3 wedges per serving)

125g mozzarella, torn into chunks. OR you can substitute

the Mozzarella with 85g of grated Cheddar.

METHOD

1. Heat oven to 200C/fan 180C/gas 6. Carefully roll the pastry out and cut into four equal rectangles. Using a sharp knife, score a 1cm border inside each rectangle. Be careful not to cut all the way through the pastry. Place on a baking tray.

2. Spread 1 tablespoon of the pesto onto each rectangle, staying inside the border. Pile on the peppers and artichokes. Cook in the oven for approx.15 mins or until the pastry is starting to brown.

3. Tear the mozzarella (or cheddar) into small chunks and place it on top of the vegetables. Return to the oven for another 5-7 mins until the pastry is golden brown and the cheese has melted. These slices are lovely served with a crisp green salad.

GRILLED VEGETABLE & FETA TART

PREP: 10 MINS   **COOK:** 40 MINS   **SERVES** 4

INGREDIENTS

2 tablespoons olive oil

1 aubergine, sliced

2 courgettes, sliced

2 red onions, cut into thick wedges

3 large sheets filo pastry

A dozen cherry tomatoes, cut into halves

A drizzle of balsamic vinegar

85g feta cheese, crumbled

1 teaspoon of dried oregano

METHOD

1. Heat oven to 220C/200C fan/gas 7. Place a 33 x 23cm baking tray in the oven to preheat. Brush a griddle pan with about 1 teaspoon of the oil and grill the aubergines until they nice char marks. Remove the aubergines to a plate and repeat the process with the courgettes and onions. You may need to add a little more oil to prevent sticking.

2. Take the preheated tray from the oven and brush with olive oil. Brush a large sheet of filo with oil, top with another sheet, add a little more oil and repeat with the final sheet. Transfer the pastry to the hot tray, use your fingers to push the pastry in the edges and corners in you need to.

3. Place the grilled vegetables on top, then season with salt and pepper. Add the cherry tomatoes with the cut sides facing up. Lastly, crumble the feta over the vegetables and drizzle the balsamic vinegar, remaining olive oil and sprinkle the oregano. Cook for about 20 mins until the pastry is golden brown and crisp.

Serve with a fresh salad.

MEDITERRANEAN FIG & MOZZARELLA SALAD

PREP: 15 MINS   **COOK:** 5 MINS **SERVES:** 6 AS A STARTER

This salad will also serve four people as a main.

INGREDIENTS

200g fine green beans ends trimmed

6 small figs cut into quarters

1 shallot thinly sliced

1 x 125g ball mozzarella, drained and torn into chunks

50g hazelnuts, toasted and chopped

A small handful of fresh basil leaves ripped

3 tablespoons olive oil

3 tablespoons balsamic vinegar

1 tablespoon of fig relish or jam

METHOD

1. Blanch the green beans in a large saucepan of salted water for 2-3 minutes. Drain the beans in a colander and rinse in cold water to stop the cooking process. Remove excess water from the beans by allowing them to drain on a paper towel or kitchen paper. Arrange the beans on a large serving platter. Top with the quartered figs, sliced shallots, mozzarella, hazelnuts, and basil.

2. In a small mixing bowl, combine the vinegar, fig jam/relish, olive oil and season with salt and pepper. Stir well to combine and drizzle over the salad just before serving.

MEDITERRANEAN FETA SALAD WITH POMEGRANATE DRESSING

PREP: 10 MINS   **COOK:** 30 MINS   **SERVES:** 8

The Pomegranate Molasses gives this salad a zesty Middle Eastern flavor

INGREDIENTS

2 red peppers
3 aubergines, medium sized
6 tablespoons olive oil
1 teaspoon cinnamon
200g green beans, blanched (or frozen beans)
1 small red onion, sliced into semi-circles
200g feta cheese, crumbled
Seeds of one pomegranate
A handful of parsley, coarsely chopped

Dressing:

1 small garlic clove, crushed
1 tablespoon lemon juice
2 tablespoon pomegranate molasses
5 tablespoon olive oil

METHOD

1. Heat oven to 200C/fan 180C/gas 6. Preheat the grill to HIGH. Cut the peppers into quarters, and deseed them.

Skin side up; place the pepper on a baking tray and grill until blackened and charred. Use tongs to place the grilled peppers into a plastic bag while still hot. Seal the bag and leave for 5 mins. When the peppers have cooled, their skins should scrape skins off easily. Discard the skins, and set peppers aside to cool completely.

2. Place the aubergines on a baking tray and drizzle with olive oil. Sprinkle with cinnamon and season with salt and pepper. Roast for approx. 25 mins or until golden and soft.

3. While the aubergines are cooking, combine all the dressing ingredients. To serve this salad, layer the aubergines, green beans, onion and peppers on a large platter. Sprinkle with the crumbled feta and pomegranate seeds. Pour the dressing all over just before serving and scatter the chopped parsley on top to finish.

MEDITERRANEAN POTATO SALAD

PREP: 10 **MINS**   **COOK:** 25 MINS   **SERVES** 4

For a low-fat version of this salad, you can substitute the mayonnaise base for cherry tomatoes, roasted red peppers, and fresh Italian herbs.

INGREDIENTS

1 tablespoon olive oil

1 small onion diced small

1 garlic clove, crushed

1 teaspoon oregano

½ x 400g can cherry tomatoes

100g roasted red pepper (from a jar is suitable)

300g new potatoes, keep whole if small, halve if larger

25g black olives, diced small

A handful of fresh basil leaves torn

METHOD

1. Heat the Olive oil in a small pan and sauté the diced onion on medium heat. Cook for 10 mins until soft and translucent. Add the crushed garlic and oregano and cook for another minute. Add the tomatoes and peppers, season well with salt and pepper. Turn the heat down to low and simmer gently for 10 mins.

2. To cook the potatoes put them in a saucepan of boiling salted water for 10-15 mins until tender. Drain well in a colander, and return to the warm saucepan. Toss the potatoes with the sauce Sprinkle the potatoes with olives and fresh basil and serve warm.

ORZO & MOZZARELLA SALAD

PREP: 10 MINS   **COOK:** 8 MINS   **SERVES** 4

Including pasta in this simple salad makes it filling enough for a main meal.

INGREDIENTS

350g orzo or another tiny pasta shape like Risoni

20g pack fresh basil

4 tablespoon olive oil

25g parmesan cheese finely grated, plus more to serve

1 garlic clove, roughly chopped

50g toasted pine nuts

290g pack bocconcini (baby mozzarella balls)

100g semi-dried tomatoes, roughly chopped

50g rocket

METHOD

1. Boil the pasta until tender according to packet instructions. Drain and rinse under cold water. Drain well again and put the cooked pasta into a large mixing bowl.

2. Rip the basil leaves including the stalks and all, and put into a food processor. Add the Olive oil, Parmesan, garlic and half the Pine Nuts. Process until a pesto-like consistency.

3. Stir the dressing through the pasta and season with salt and pepper. Don't worry if the dressing seems too thick, just keep stirring and it will eventually coat all the pasta. Add the bocconcini, semi-dried tomatoes and a handful of the rocket; leave a little aside for garnish. When you're ready to serve, top with a little extra Parmesan and the remaining Pine Nuts and Rocket.

ROASTED AUBERGINE WITH BULGUR & ZESTY DRESSING

PREP: 10 MINS   **COOK:** 30 MINS   **SERVES** 4

This meal is high in fiber, super tasty and full of Middle Eastern flavor.

INGREDIENTS

- 2 aubergines, cut in half lengthways

- 6 tablespoons olive oil

- 250g bulgur wheat

- 2 large onions, finely sliced

- 1 tablespoon ground cumin

- 400g can chickpeas, rinsed well and drained

- Handful each of fresh coriander and mint, chopped roughly

- 1 garlic clove, crushed

- Zest and juice of 1 lemon

METHOD

1. Heat oven to 220C/200C fan/gas 7. Score a criss-cross pattern in the aubergine with the tip of a sharp knife. Place in a roasting tray and brush with 2 tablespoons of Olive oil. Season with salt and pepper and then roast for 30 mins.

2. Meanwhile, put the Bulgur into a saucepan with 1 liter of water. Bring to the boil, and lower the heat to simmer for 15 mins. Cook the onions in 1 tablespoon of Olive oil until soft and translucent. Add the ground Cumin and cook for another minute. Drain the Bulgur well and stir into the onions. Add the chickpeas, season well with salt and pepper. Stir to combine.

3. Combine the remaining oil with the fresh herbs, garlic, lemon zest, juice, and seasoning. To serve, divide the Bulgar between the plates. Place an Aubergine half on top, and drizzle the dressing over the top.

CRISPY GREEK-STYLE PIE

PREP: 10 MINS   **COOK:** 30 MINS   **SERVES** 4

This crispy pie is a fail-safe recipe to add to your collection. You can add whatever vegetables you have in the kitchen to make your own creation.

INGREDIENTS

200g baby spinach Leaves

175g jar sundried tomato in oil

100g feta cheese, crumbled

2 eggs

½ 250g pack filo pastry

METHOD

1. Heat oven to 180C/fan 160C/gas 4. Put the spinach into a large pan and wilt it with a couple of tablespoons of hot water. Drain in a sieve and squeeze out any excess water when cool enough to handle. Roughly chop the Spinach. Roughly chop the tomatoes and put into a mixing bowl along with the spinach, feta, and eggs. Stir until well combined.

2. Unroll the filo pastry and cover with some damp sheets of kitchen towel to prevent it drying out. Use a pastry brush and liberally brush the pastry sheet with sundried tomato oil. Drape oil-side down in a 22cm spring-form cake tin. The pastry should hang over the sides. Continue this process with another two sheets of pastry so you have three in total. Spoon the egg mixture into the cake tin. Fold over the pastry edges and pull/scrunch together so all the filling is covered. Brush the top of the pastry with a little more oil.

3. Place the pie into the oven for 30 mins until golden brown. Serve the pie sliced into wedges, with a crisp salad.

VEGETARIAN CASSEROLE

PREP: 10 MINS   **COOK:** 40 MINS   **SERVES** 4

Packed full of vegetables, this stew is healthy and delicious.
Cleaning up will be a breeze with this one-pot stew.

INGREDIENTS

1 tablespoon olive oil

1 onion, diced

3 garlic cloves, sliced thinly

1 teaspoon smoked paprika

½ teaspoon ground cumin

1 tablespoon dried thyme

3 medium carrots sliced

2 medium sticks of celery, finely sliced

1 red pepper, chopped

1 yellow pepper, chopped

2 x 400g cans diced Tomatoes

250ml vegetable stock

2 courgettes, sliced thickly

2 sprigs fresh thyme

250g cooked lentils

METHOD

1. Heat 1 tablespoon of olive oil on medium heat in a large, heavy-based pan. Add the finely chopped onion and cook gently for 5 – 10 mins until soft and translucent.

2. Add the sliced garlic cloves, paprika, cumin, dried thyme, carrots, celery, and the red and yellow peppers. Cook for 5 minutes stirring occasionally.

3. Add the two cans of diced tomatoes, the vegetable stock, sliced courgettes and 2 sprigs fresh thyme and cook for 20 - 25 minutes.

4. Take out the fresh thyme sprigs and discard. Stir in the cooked lentils and bring back to a simmer to heat them through. Serve this stew over mashed vegetables, wild rice or quinoa.

POTATO FRITTATA WITH PESTO & GOAT'S CHEESE

PREP: 10 MINS COOK: 20 - 25 MINS SERVES 4

Potatoes combine beautifully with pesto and goat's cheese in this tasty Spanish Omelette. It's important to use an ovenproof frying pan to make this dish.

INGREDIENTS

4 medium potatoes, thinly sliced

1 garlic clove, finely chopped

8 large eggs

1 tablespoon olive oil

100g pack soft goat's cheese, sliced

3 tablespoons of basil pesto

A handful of rocket

METHOD

1. Heat oven to 220C/200C fan/gas 7. Bring a pot of salted water to the boil and cook the potato slices till they are just tender. Drain well using a colander.

2. Whisk the eggs and garlic together and season with salt and pepper. When the potatoes have cooled, add them to the egg mixture.

3. Heat the olive oil on a low heat in a large frying pan, and pour in the egg and potato mixture. Cook for 5 minutes, or until two-thirds of the frittata is set. Ensuring that your frypan is ovenproof, finish cooking the frittata in the oven for 10-15 mins and cooked through.

4. Place the sliced goat's cheese around the edge of the frittata. Drizzle the pesto on top as well. Garnish with the Rocket and serve with salad and crusty bread.

MINTED COURGETTE SALAD

PREP: 10 MINS, PLus 10 Mins marinating **SERVES** 8

This salad made look simple, but it's bursting with flavor. Serve it with a Mediterranean tasting plate, or your favorite meat dish.

INGREDIENTS

½ red onion, thinly sliced

Zest and juice of 1 lemon

2 courgettes

A large handful of mint, shredded

2 tablespoons of olive oil

METHOD

1. Mix the onion and lemon juice together with some salt and pepper; leave to the side for 10 mins. When ready to serve this salad or dish up your meal, slice the courgettes into thin ribbons using a vegetable peeler. Toss all the ingredients together in a bowl and combine well. Serve immediately.

Soups

YELLOW GAZPACHO

PREP: 5 MINS   **COOK**: 25 MINS   **SERVES** 8

This bright and vibrant soup is served chilled.

INGREDIENTS

1 ½ cups cucumber, peeled, deseeded and diced

1 cup red onion, diced

1 cup yellow bell pepper, cut into chunks

6 tablespoons white wine vinegar

1 tablespoon olive oil

6 large yellow tomatoes, peeled and deseeded

METHOD

1. In a large mixing bowl combine the cucumber, onion, peppers, white wine vinegar and olive oil.

2. Season well with salt and pepper and mix well.

3. Using a food processor, whizz the vegetables until smooth, you may need to do this in batches. Transfer the puree to a clean bowl.

4. Cover the puree and chill in the fridge.

5. Serve the gazpacho with crusty bread and olive oil and balsamic for dipping.

CHICKPEA, TOMATO, AND PASTA SOUP

PREP: 5 MINS   **COOK**: 25 MINS   **SERVES** 4

This vegetarian soup is a great alternative to meat dishes. It's loaded with spices and beans and the pasta turns it into a filling meal.

INGREDIENTS

2 teaspoons olive oil

1 cup diced onion

1 cup of water

500mL chicken or vegetable stock

¼ teaspoon ground cumin

¼ teaspoon ground cinnamon

1 400g can chickpeas, rinsed and drained

1 400g can diced tomatoes, undrained

½ cup uncooked macaroni

2 tablespoons fresh Italian parsley, chopped

METHOD

1. Heat a large saucepan over medium-high heat and add the olive. Sauté the onion for 3 minutes until soft and translucent.

2. Add the cumin and cinnamon and lightly toast the spices for another minute.

3. Pour in the stock, water, canned tomatoes, macaroni, and chickpeas. Season well with salt and pepper.

4. Bring mixture to a boil, cover and reduce heat to a low simmer for 10-15 minutes until pasta is tender, stirring occasionally.

5. Stir in chopped parsley and serve hot.

LENTIL AND SPINACH SOUP WITH POMEGRANATE MOLASSES

PREP: 5 MINS   **COOK**: 25 MINS   **SERVES** 8

INGREDIENTS

6 cups of water

1 ½ cups dried lentils

2 garlic cloves, crushed

1 bay leaf

1 cinnamon stick

4 cups diced aubergine, approx. 4. Cut into chunks

1 onion, chopped finely

1 thyme sprig

1 tablespoon extra virgin olive oil

4 cups less-sodium beef broth, divided

½ cup fresh Italian parsley, chopped

1 (6-ounce) package baby spinach

8 teaspoons pomegranate molasses

½ cup thinly sliced bottled roasted red bell pepper

METHOD

1. Put 6 cups of water into a large pot over medium-high heat. Add the garlic, cinnamon, lentils and bay leaf. Bring to the boil, then reduce heat to a simmer for 20 mins and remove from heat. Discard bay leaf and cinnamon.

2. Preheat oven to 450°. Place the eggplant, onion, and thyme in a baking dish. Drizzle with the olive oil and toss to coat. Bake 30 minutes, stirring once halfway.

3. Add 1 cup of stock to the baking dish, and return to the oven for another 10 minutes. Discard thyme and then add the eggplant mixture to pot with the lentils. Stir in the remaining 3 cups of stock and add the parsley.

4. Bring to a boil over medium-high heat. Then cover; reduce heat to a simmer for 10 minutes. Remove from heat.

5. Add spinach and stir to incorporate as the spinach wilts. Season well with salt and pepper.

6. Serve in bowls with a drizzle of pomegranate molasses and a tablespoon of the roasted bell peppers.

MEDITERRANEAN FISH STEW

PREP: 5 MINS   **COOK**: 25 MINS   **SERVES** 4

INGREDIENTS

1 tablespoon olive oil

½ cup onion, finely chopped

2 garlic cloves, crushed

2 cups green beans cut in 1" lengths

1 small carrot, thinly sliced

500mL chicken stock

1 400g can cannellini beans, rinsed and drained

1 400g diced tomatoes, undrained

1 cup uncooked medium pasta, like shells

2 tablespoons fresh basil, finely chopped

1 tablespoon fresh oregano, finely chopped

2 tablespoons tomato paste

400g skinless halibut fillets cut into 1-inch pieces

1/4 cup Parmesan cheese, grated

METHOD

1. Place a large saucepan over medium to high heat and add the olive oil. Sauté the onion and garlic in the oil pan for 3 minutes. Add green beans, cannellini beans, stock, carrot, and tomatoes and bring to a boil.

2. Add the pasta then reduce heat and cover. Simmer for approx. 12 minutes or until pasta is tender.

3. Stir in basil, oregano, tomato paste, and season well with salt and pepper.

4. Add the fish to the pot, and cook for approx. 3 minutes.

5. Serve hot in bowls with a sprinkle with Parmesan cheese.

ITALIAN SAUSAGE MINESTRONE

PREP: 20 MINS   **COOK: 50 MINS**   **SERVES 6**

This hearty soup is a meal within itself! Serve with crusty bread for extra crunch.

INGREDIENTS

500g Italian sausages, casings removed

2 tablespoons olive oil

2 celery stalks, roughly chopped

1 medium onion, roughly chopped

5 garlic cloves, crushed

3 cups green beans, trimmed and cut into 1" lengths

350g frozen artichoke hearts, thawed

2 400g cans diced tomatoes

1 teaspoon dried oregano

6 cups beef stock

½ cup small pasta such as macaroni or small shells

1 400g can chickpeas

1 cup parsley leaves, chopped

7 large fresh basil leaves, torn

¼ cup Parmesan, grated

METHOD

1. Heat a pan on medium-high heat and add 1 tablespoon of olive oil. Brown the sausage until it is fully cooked, remove and set aside.

2. In a large pot heat 1 tablespoon of olive oil and sauté the onion and celery for 2-3 minutes. Add in garlic and sauté for another minute.

3. Add the green beans, artichoke hearts, canned tomatoes, dried oregano and season with salt and pepper. Cook on medium-high heat for 5 minutes.

4. Now add the cooked sausage and stock and cook for another 10 minutes, stirring occasionally

5. Lower the heat to low, cover and simmer for another 15 minutes.

6. Add the pasta and chickpeas, bring the heat back to high and cook uncovered for another 8-9 minutes until pasta is tender.

7. Remove from heat and stir in the fresh basil and parsley. Serve in bowls topped with Parmesan.

GREEN CHILI CHICKEN AND BEAN SOUP

PREP: 10 MINS   **COOK**: 30 MINS   **SERVES** 6-8

INGREDIENTS

3 large chicken breasts cut into chunks

3 tablespoons olive oil

1 onion, finely diced

3 cloves garlic, crushed

1 tablespoon ground cumin

1 teaspoon dried oregano

4 cups chicken stock `

2 cups of water

1 jar Salsa Verde

1 180g can diced green chilies

2 400g cans navy beans, drained and rinsed

METHOD

1. Heat the olive oil in a large pan over medium heat. Add the chicken and brown all over. Add the onion and garlic and sauté for 2 minutes with the chicken. Once the chicken is mostly browned, add onion and garlic and sauté for 2 minutes with chicken. Season well with salt and pepper.

2. Add the cumin and oregano and stir to combine.

3. Pour in the water and use a wooden spoon to deglaze the pan and scrape up all the flavors from browning the chicken.

4. Add the jar of Salsa Verde, beans and the diced green chilies.

5. Lastly, add the stock. Simmer on a low heat for 20-30 minutes.

6. Serve hot in bowls, with dried chili flakes and a dollop of sour cream if desired.

MOROCCAN CHICKPEA & LENTIL SOUP

PREP: 15 MINS   **COOK**: 1 HR 45 MINS **SERVES** 6

INGREDIENTS

3 tablespoons olive oil

450g beef or lamb, cut into ½" cubes

1 large onion, diced

2 stalks celery, diced

2 cloves garlic, crushed

2 teaspoons fresh ginger, grated

400g can diced tomatoes

¼ cup tomato paste

2 teaspoons of both ground cumin & sweet paprika

1 teaspoon of both ground coriander & smoked paprika

1 ½ teaspoon ground turmeric

½ teaspoon ground cinnamon

1 tablespoon preserved lemon, minced

8 cups beef or lamb stock

400g can chickpeas, rinsed and drained

¾ cup dried lentils

¼ cup long grain rice

1/3 cup each of green and black olives, sliced

GARNISH

1/3 cup fresh cilantro, chopped

1/3 cup fresh parsley, chopped

Lemon wedges for serving

METHOD

1. Heat the oil in a pot over medium-high heat and brown the meat. Transfer the meat to a plate and set aside.

2. Add the onions and cook until soft and golden, 6-8 minutes. Add the celery, garlic, and ginger and cook for another 2 minutes. Add the tomatoes, tomato paste, spices, preserved lemon and let the mixture simmer for a couple of minutes.

3. Return the meat to the pot with the chickpeas and lentils. Add the stock, bring to a boil, cover and simmer on a low heat for 1 hour. Add the rice, cover and continue to simmer for another 30 minutes stirring occasionally.

4. Stir in the olives, cilantro, and parsley and simmer for another 5 minutes. Season with salt and pepper.

5. Garnish with some chopped fresh cilantro and celery leaves. Serve with lemon wedges.

MEDITERRANEAN QUINOA SOUP

PREP: 5 MINS   **COOK:** 25 MINS   **SERVES** 4

INGREDIENTS

1 small onion, finely diced

5 garlic cloves, crushed

3 medium carrots, sliced into thin rounds

1 tablespoon olive oil

½ cup dry red quinoa

6 cups vegetable stock

400g can of garbanzo beans

1 lemon

4 cups spinach

Pesto and marinated artichokes for garnish

METHOD

1. In a large pot on medium heat, sauté the onion, garlic, and carrots with 1 tablespoon of olive oil for 5 minutes until lightly cooked.

2. Add the dry red quinoa to the pot and sauté for 1 minute stirring constantly. Pour in the stock and beans.

3. Turn the heat down to medium-low and simmer for 20 minutes, stirring several times to ensure the quinoa doesn't stick to the bottom of the pot.

4. Remove from the heat and stir in the juice of one lemon.

5. To serve, divide the spinach between four bowls and top with the soup. Garnish with a dollop of pesto and the artichokes.

KALE, CANNELLINI AND FARRO STEW

PREP: 15 MINS   **COOK:** 45 MINS   **SERVES** 6

Farro is an ancient whole grain that belongs to the wheat family.

INGREDIENTS

2 tablespoons olive oil

2 medium carrots, diced

1 small onion, diced

2 celery stalks, diced

4 cloves garlic, crushed

5 cups vegetable stock

200g can diced tomatoes

1 cup farro, rinsed

1 teaspoon dried oregano

1 bay leaf

1 handful of parsley leaves and sprigs

4 cups kale, chopped

400g can cannellini beans, drained and rinsed

1 tablespoon fresh lemon juice

Feta cheese, crumbled for serving

METHOD

1. Heat the olive oil in a large pot over medium-high heat. Sauté the carrot, onion, and celery for 3 minutes. Add the garlic and cook for another minute.

2. Pour in the stock, tomatoes, farro, oregano, bay leaf and season with salt and pepper.

3. Add parsley and bring soup to a boil. Reduce heat just below medium.

4. Cover and simmer 20 minutes. Remove parsley and discard. Add chopped kale and cook 10 - 15 minutes, check that both the farro and kale are tender.

5. Add the cannellini beans and allow them to heat through, for approx. 2 minutes. Remove bay leaf, stir in lemon juice.

6. Add some additional stock or water to thin the soup as the farro may absorb quite a bit of the liquid. Serve warm topping each serving with crumbled feta.

MEDITERRANEAN TOMATO SOUP

PREP: 10 MINS   **COOK:** 30 MINS   **SERVES** 4

INGREDIENTS

2 green (spring) onions, sliced finely

2 tablespoons olive oil

1 garlic clove, crushed

400g can diced tomatoes

1 tablespoon sun-dried tomato paste

2 cups vegetable stock

1 teaspoon ground paprika

1 courgette, dices

100g cherry tomatoes cut into quarters

400g white beans, rinsed and drained

6 sprigs thyme, chopped

1 pinch sugar

METHOD

1. Heat the olive oil in a large saucepan on medium-high heat. Add the spring onions and the garlic, sauté for 1 minute. Add the courgette and cook for 5 mins.

2. Add the canned tomatoes, tomato paste, stock, beans, thyme, and paprika. Bring to the boil and then reduce heat to low. Cover and simmer for 20 mins, stirring occasionally.

3. Remove from the heat and allow to cool down for a few minutes. Blend the soup in batches using a food processor or immersion/stick blender.

4. Return soup to the saucepan and low heat. Stir in the sugar and season with salt and pepper. Serves hot in soup bowls topped with a few fresh cherry tomatoes for garnish.

GREEK CHICKPEA SOUP WITH LEMON

PREP: 10MINS+ overnight   **COOK:** 2-3 HRS   **SERVES** 4

Despite only having seven ingredients, this Greek chickpea soup packs quite a flavor punch. Serve with extra lemon wedges for additional acidity.

INGREDIENTS

1 cup dried chickpeas soaked in water for 12-18 hours

1 onion, chopped into pieces about 1/4 inch

4 tablespoons olive oil

1 teaspoon dried oregano

1 teaspoon dried parsley

8 cups of water

¼ cup fresh squeezed lemon juice

METHOD

1. Inspect the dried chickpeas and discard any small stones or debris. Put the beans in a pan and cover with cold water. Leave to soak for 12-18 hours. When ready to make soup, drain beans and discard soaking water.

2. Heat 2 tablespoons of olive oil in a soup pot over medium to high heat. Add onion and sauté for about 5 minutes, until onion is soft and translucent. It's important to the presentation of this soup that your onions do not brown.

3. Add the oregano, parsley, and water and bring to a low simmer. Cover the pan and simmer until the beans are very tender. This will take anywhere between 2-3 hours.

4. When beans are soft, use a stick blender to puree the mixture until all ingredients are completely blended and smooth. After the soup is pureed, season with salt and fresh pepper to taste. Stir in the lemon juice and 2 T of the olive oil. Serve hot, with a bit more olive oil drizzled on the top of each serving.

MEDITERRANEAN POTATO SOUP

PREP: 10 MINS   **COOK**: 25 MINS   **SERVES** 4

Not only is this soup incredibly filling and tasty, but it is extremely cost effective too!

INGREDIENTS

2 teaspoons olive oil

1 clove garlic minced

1 small onion, chopped finely

4 cups chicken or vegetable stock

3 medium red potatoes, unpeeled and cut into cubes

3 medium carrots, sliced in rounds

2 teaspoons Italian seasoning

400g can red kidney beans, rinsed and drained

1 cup whole wheat noodles, uncooked

2 cups fresh spinach

¼ cup Parmesan cheese, grated

METHOD

1. Heat the oil in a soup pot and sauté the garlic and onion for 3-4 minutes.

2. Add the stock, water, potatoes, carrots and season well with salt and pepper. Cover and bring to a boil.

3. Reduce heat and simmer 15 minutes.

4. Add kidney beans and noodles, and bring to boil again, cook until noodles are soft.

5. Remove from heat. Add spinach and stir gently until wilted.

6. Serve into bowls and top with Parmesan cheese.

ROASTED TOMATO & MASCARPONE SOUP

PREP: 15 MINS   **COOK**: 1 HR, 20 MINS   **SERVES** 4

This creamy Italian soup is big on flavor and the ultimate comfort food for a cool winter night. This soup also freezes really well. Store in airtight containers in your freezer for up to a month.

INGREDIENTS

1kg tomatoes, very ripe

Pinch of caster sugar

1 tablespoon balsamic vinegar

3 tablespoon olive oil

1 large onion, chopped

1 carrot, finely chopped

1 sprig of fresh thyme and 2 bay leaves tied together

2 garlic cloves, chopped

1 tablespoon tomato purée

600ml vegetable stock

2 tablespoon Mascarpone cheese (or cream)

METHOD

1. Heat oven to 170C/150C fan/gas 3 - 4. Prepare a large bowl with ice water and set aside. Bring a saucepan of water and bring to the boil. Using a sharp knife cut a small cross into the bottom of each tomato. Plunge into boiling water (a few tomatoes at a time) for 10 seconds. Use a slotted spoon to lift out and place in the iced water. Drain and peel the tomatoes. Slice the tomatoes in half and place cut side up on a baking tray. Season with salt and pepper. Sprinkle the tomatoes with the pinch of caster sugar. Drizzle the tomatoes with the Balsamic Vinegar and a tablespoon of Olive oil. Roast for an hour and set aside.

2. Heat the rest of the Olive oil in a large pot and sauté the carrots and onion on medium heat for about 10 mins until very soft. Add the bay leave and thyme, and the garlic and cook for another minute. Add the tomato purée. Pour in the roasted tomatoes and any liquid from the roasting pan. Add the stock and season well with salt and pepper. Increase the heat to bring the soup to the boil, then lower the heat and simmer for 10 mins.

3. Remove the tied herbs with tongs and discard. Take the soup off the heat and add the Mascarpone Cheese. Use a hand blender to whizz the soup into a consistency that you're happy with. To serve, top the soup with a sprig of thyme and a drizzle of good quality olive oil.

CHUNKY MEDITERRANEAN VEGGIE SOUP

PREP: 10 MINS   **COOK**: 25 MINS   **SERVES** 4

This soup is a fantastic way to use up grilled vegetables. It's low in calories too, so enjoy this one guilt-free.

INGREDIENTS

400g leftover grilled vegetables cut into chunks – use peppers, courgettes, aubergines. Spinach, carrot, and celery will also work well and don't need to be grilled beforehand.

1 large Onion, finely diced

2 garlic cloves, crushed

Handful fresh basil leaves

400g can diced tomato

1 reduced-salt vegetable stock cube

50g ricotta

METHOD

1. Heat a large saucepan or stockpot on high heat. Put the chopped vegetable and garlic in the pot. Cook, stirring, over high heat for 5 minutes. Rip up the basil leaves; add the tomatoes and the stock cube. Using the empty tomato can add two cans of water. Simmer until all vegetables are cooked through and tender. Blend with a hand blender if you would like a smooth consistency, or leave your soup chunky if you prefer.

2. To serve, ladle the hot soup into bowls. Top with the crumbled Ricotta and serve with warm crusty bread.

Seafood Dishes

SPICY SHRIMP WITH CAULIFLOWER & ARUGULA

PREP: 10 MINS   **COOK**: 20 MINS   **SERVES** 4

INGREDIENTS

500g shrimp, peeled and deveined

1 tablespoon paprika

2 teaspoons garlic powder

½ teaspoon cayenne pepper

2 tablespoons olive oil

1 tablespoon unsalted butter

4 cups cauliflower, grated finely for cauliflower 'rice'

1 cup milk

½ cup goat cheese, crumbled

3 garlic cloves, crushed

4 cups baby arugula

METHOD

1. In a ziplock bag combine the paprika, garlic powder, and cayenne. Add the shrimp to the bag and seal. Shake the bag gently ensuring all the shrimp are coated with the spices. Put in the refrigerator.

2. Melt the butter over medium heat in a large pan. Add the cauliflower rice and cook for 2 to 3 minutes until slightly softened.

3. Stir in half of the milk and bring to a simmer. Continue to simmer, stirring occasionally, until the cauliflower absorbs some of the milk, 6 to 8 minutes.

4. Add the remaining milk and simmer until the mixture is thick and creamy, 10 minutes more. Stir in the goat cheese and season well with salt and pepper. Remove from the heat, but keep warm for serving.

5. In a large skillet, heat 1 tablespoon of olive oil over medium heat. Add the garlic and sauté until fragrant, 1 minute. Add the arugula and sauté until wilted, 3 to 4 minutes. Season with salt and pepper. Transfer to a plate.

6. In the same skillet, heat the remaining 1 tablespoon of olive oil over medium heat. Add the shrimp and sauté until fully cooked approx. 4 to 5 minutes. Season with salt and pepper.

7. To serve, divide the cauliflower rice among four plates and top each with a quarter of the arugula and a quarter of the shrimp. Serve immediately.

BAKED GINGER SALMON

PREP: 10 MINS   **COOK: 20 MINS**   **SERVES 4**

Salmon is rich in Omega 3 oils, which are essential for heart health.

INGREDIENTS

1 teaspoon sesame oil

2 tablespoons soy sauce

2 tablespoons grated fresh ginger

1 teaspoon garlic powder

2 tablespoons honey

Pinch of red pepper flakes

2 large zucchini, halved lengthwise and thinly sliced

1 red onion, halved and thinly sliced

1 lime, quartered

4 x 175g skinless salmon fillets

4 teaspoons sesame seeds

METHOD

1. Preheat the oven to 350°F. Cut four squares of parchment paper, or baking paper. Fold each square in half to make a crease and unfold. Set aside.

2. Combine the sesame oil and soy sauce in a small bowl. Add the ginger, garlic powder, honey, and red pepper flakes and lightly whisk to combine.

3. Take on a square of baking paper and place a quarter of the zucchini in an even layer on one half of the paper, close to the crease. Top with a quarter of the red onion. Squeeze one of the lime wedges over the vegetables.

4. Place one salmon fillet on top of the vegetables. Drizzle a quarter of the soy sauce mixture over the salmon and sprinkle with a teaspoon of sesame seeds.

5. Fold the empty side of the paper over the salmon and then fold all three open edges toward the salmon, making several creases folds and ensuring the package is sealed.

6. Repeat the process with the remaining ingredients and baking paper. Place the four parcels on a baking tray and cook for 16 to 18 minutes.

7. Remove the parcels from the oven. Using a large spatula transfer to four plates, still in the paper. Cut slits in the top of the paper, and serve immediately.

GREEK SHRIMP FARRO BOWLS

PREP: 10 MINS   COOK: 20 MINS   SERVES 4

INGREDIENTS

500g shrimp, peeled and deveined

3 tablespoons olive oil

2 cloves garlic, crushed

1 lemon

2 teaspoons fresh dill, chopped

1 tablespoon fresh oregano, chopped

½ teaspoon smoked paprika

½ teaspoon of sea salt

¼ teaspoon black pepper

1 cup dry farro

2 bell peppers, deseeded and sliced thickly

2 medium-sized courgettes, sliced into rounds

250g cherry tomatoes halved

¼ cup black olives, diced

4 tablespoon plain Greek yogurt

METHOD

1. Combine the olive oil, garlic, lemon, dill, oregano, paprika, salt, and pepper in a small bowl. Mix well. Place the shrimp in a ziplock bag, and pour ¾ of the herb and spice mixture over the shrimp ensuring it is all well coated. Leave to marinade 10 minutes in the refrigerator.

2. Cook farro as directed by the packet instructions. Then heat a frying pan or non-stick skillet over medium heat. Cook shrimp for 2-3 minutes per side, and transfer to a plate.

3. Cook the vegetables in batches in the same skillet or pan. Cook 5-6 minutes, until softened. Repeat with remaining vegetables.

4. Divide cooked farro among 4 bowls. Top with shrimp, grilled vegetables, olives or beans, and tomatoes. Drizzle reserved marinade over the top. Serve with a tablespoon of Greek yogurt and extra lemon wedges if desired.

MEDITERRANEAN COD WITH KALE & FENNEL

PREP: 5 MINS   **COOK:** 30 MINS   **SERVES** 4

INGREDIENTS

2 tablespoon olive oil

1 small onion, sliced

2 cups fennel, sliced

3 garlic cloves, crushed

1 400g can diced tomato

1 cup fresh tomatoes, diced

2 cups kale, shredded

½ cup of water

A pinch of cayenne pepper

½ teaspoon dried oregano

1 cup black olives

600g cod divided into 4 portions

1 teaspoon orange zest

Fresh oregano fennel fronds, orange zest, olive oil for garnish if required.

METHOD

1. Heat a large skillet over medium heat. Add the olive oil and cook onion, fennel, and garlic together for 8 minutes. Season with salt and pepper.

2. Pour in the canned diced tomato; add the fresh tomato, kale, and water. Stir well and cook for 12 minutes. Add crushed red pepper, oregano, and olives.

3. Prepare the cod by seasoning with salt, pepper, and the orange zest. Bury fish into kale and tomato mixture. Cover pan, turn heat to low and cook for 10 minutes.

4. Remove from heat, and garnish with fennel fronds, more fresh oregano, more orange zest, and a drizzle of olive oil on top. Serve immediately.

MEDITERRANEAN COUSCOUS WITH TUNA & PEPPERONCINI

PREP: 5 MINS   **COOK: 10 MINS**   **SERVES 4**

Pepperoncini is the Italian name for red chili peppers. If you like your meal spicy, add extra fresh chili as a garnish.

INGREDIENTS

1 cup chicken stock

1¼ cups couscous

285 cans of oil-packed tuna

250g cherry tomatoes halved

½ cup pepperoncini, sliced

⅓ cup fresh parsley, chopped

¼ cup capers

Extra-virgin olive oil, for serving

1 lemon, quartered

METHOD

1. Bring the stock to the boil in a saucepan over medium heat. Once boiling, remove the saucepan from the heat and stir in the couscous. Cover and set it aside for 10 minutes.

2. Toss together the tuna, tomatoes, pepperoncini, parsley, and capers in a medium sized mixing bowl.

3. Fluff the couscous with a fork, season well with salt and pepper. Divide the couscous between four bowls and top with the tuna mixture. Drizzle with olive oil and serve with fresh lemon wedges.

ROASTED MEDITERRANEAN SHRIMP WITH QUINOA

PREP: 10 MINS　　　**COOK: 8 MINS**　　　**SERVES 4**

INGREDIENTS

¼ cup extra-virgin olive oil

2 tablespoon red wine vinegar

The zest of 1 lemon

2 tablespoons fresh lemon juice

2 large garlic cloves, crushed

2 teaspoons dried oregano

½ teaspoon red pepper flakes or chili flakes

800g shrimp, peeled and deveined

250g cooked quinoa

METHOD

1. Preheat oven to 400 degrees F. Excluding the quinoa and shrimp, whisk all the ingredients together in a small mixing bowl until well combined and emulsified.

2. In a large mixing bowl, marinate peeled and deveined shrimp with one-quarter of vinaigrette. Set the remainder of the sauce aside to use later.

3. Line a baking sheet with foil and spread the shrimp out in an even layer. Season with salt and pepper.

4. Roast shrimp in the oven for 6-8 minutes or until just cooked through and light pink.

5. Remove shrimp from oven and drizzle the remaining vinaigrette.

6. Serve shrimp immediately over cooked quinoa.

SAUTÉED SHRIMP WITH FENNEL

PREP: 5 MINS   COOK: 25 MINS   SERVES 4

Don't underestimate the simplicity of this dish. It's packed full of flavor and juicy seared shrimp. Serve with couscous, over pasta or with a salad for a simple and nutritious meal.

INGREDIENTS

1 tablespoon olive oil

500g shrimp peeled and deveined

2 tablespoons capers, rinsed

¼ cup crumbled feta cheese

1 large fennel bulb, cored and cut into 2" long strips

1 400g can diced tomatoes

1 teaspoon dried oregano

METHOD

1. Heat oil in a large skillet over medium heat. Add fennel strips and cook, stirring occasionally until they start to brown, approx. 8 minutes.

2. Stir in the tomatoes and oregano. Cook while stirring with a wooden spoon, and scraping up any browned bits for approx. 1 minute.

3. Add shrimp and cook, stirring occasionally, until pink and just cooked through. This should take approx. 4 minutes.

4. Stir in capers and season well with salt and pepper. Serve immediately sprinkled with feta.

SHRIMP WITH WHOLE WHEAT SPAGHETTI

PREP: 15 MINS   **COOK: 10 MINS**   **SERVES 4**

INGREDIENTS

250g whole-wheat spaghetti noodles, uncooked
1 tablespoon olive oil

5 cloves garlic, crushed

500g shrimp, peeled and deveined

2 lemons

2 cups tomato pasta sauce or passata

¼ cup artichoke hearts, oil packed and drained

¼ cup black olives, pitted and sliced in half

1 tablespoon of capers

¼ cup feta cheese, crumbled

METHOD

1. Bring a large pot of salted water to the boil. Cook pasta according to packet instructions. Drain and set aside.

2. Heat olive oil in a non-stick pan or skillet over medium heat. Add garlic and cook 1-2 minutes, until lightly browned. Stir in shrimp and cook 6-8 minutes, or until opaque white. Squeeze juice from 2 lemons into the pan and then remove from heat.

3. In a large mixing bowl, combine the cooked pasta with the pasta sauce. Divide into four bowls. Top with shrimp, artichoke hearts, capers, olives and sprinkle with feta.

GRILLED SALMON WITH SALSA

PREP: 10 MINS   COOK: 15 MINS   SERVES 2

The salsa used in the recipe is incredibly versatile. Use it to accompany meats, as a bruschetta topping or on an antipasto platter.

INGREDIENTS

> 2 salmon fillets
> 1 teaspoon dill weed

> **Mediterranean Salsa:**

> ½ cup cherry tomatoes, quartered

> ¼ black olives, chopped

> ¼ green olives, chopped

> 1 clove garlic, crushed

> 2 tablespoons fresh oregano, stripped from stems

> 2 tablespoons chives, finely diced

> ½ teaspoon smoked paprika

> 1 tablespoon extra virgin olive oil

METHOD

1. Put salmon in a grill basket or on a mesh grill pan. Sprinkle with dill and season with salt and pepper.

2. Grill salmon for 10 – 12 minutes depending on thickness. Salmon should be opaque but slightly pink in the center.

3. To make the salsa, combine all ingredients and mix well. Leave the salsa to sit for 10 minutes to let the flavors infuse.

4. Serve the salmon with the salsa and a salad or seasonal vegetables.

MEDITERRANEAN FISH PACKETS

PREP: 10 MINS   **COOK:** 15 MINS   **SERVES** 2

INGREDIENTS

4 sheets of foil or parchment paper

1 courgette, sliced into ¼" rounds (at least 8 pieces)

1 onion, thinly sliced

4 teaspoons minced garlic (about 3 large cloves)

1 400g can stewed tomato slices

600g cod or other firm-fleshed white fish, cut into 4

pieces

4 tablespoons crumbled reduced-fat feta cheese

1 teaspoon each dried basil, oregano, and pepper

4 teaspoons olive oil

METHOD

1. Preheat oven to high (450)

2. Lay out the 4 pieces of foil. To one side of each piece of foil, layer the courgette, sliced onions, two tomato slices and a sprinkle of garlic powder.

3. Place the fish on top and sprinkle with crumbled feta. Sprinkle each portion with each of basil and oregano. Season with salt and pepper, and a drizzle of olive oil. Fold the foil over the fish scrunch up the side to seal well.

4. Bake in the oven for 15-20 minutes. Remove from the oven and allow to rest for 5 minutes.

5. Place each foil parcel on a separate plate to serve. Cut a slit in the top of the parcel, and serve with lemon wedges if desired.

GRILLED TUNA WITH OLIVE RELISH

PREP: 5 MINS   **COOK:** 20 MINS   **SERVES** 4

INGREDIENTS

TUNA

⅛ teaspoon salt

Freshly ground pepper, to taste

800g tuna steak, trimmed and cut into 6 portions

1 tablespoon olive oil plus lemon

OLIVE RELISH

½ cup finely chopped fresh parsley

⅓ cup black olives, chopped and pitted

¼ cup celery, finely chopped

1 small clove garlic, minced

½ teaspoon dried oregano

1 tablespoon lemon juice

1 teaspoon extra-virgin olive oil

METHOD

1. To prepare olive relish: Combine parsley, olives, celery, garlic, oregano, lemon juice, oil, salt and pepper in a small bowl.

2. To grill tuna: Preheat grill to medium-high. Rub tuna all over with olive oil and season with salt and pepper. Grill the tuna until seared on both sides and just cooked through, approx. 4 minutes per side.

3. Serve with Olive Relish and lemon wedges.

SEAFOOD CEVICHE

PREP: 20 MINS   COOK: -   SERVES 4

INGREDIENTS

400g shrimp peeled and deveined

400g tilapia or cod, baked and shredded

200g mini scallops cooked

¼ teaspoon cayenne pepper (optional)

¼ cup fresh lime juice

1 cup corn kernels about 3-4 cobs, blanched or canned

corn

2 Roma tomatoes, chopped

½ cup cilantro, finely chopped

2 jalapeños one finely chopped, one finely sliced

¼ cup black olives, chopped

¼ cup olive oil

3-4 limes for garnish

METHOD

1. Place the three types of seafood in a large mixing bowl.

2. Season with salt and pepper and cayenne pepper; add the lime juice and mix well.

3. Add the corn, tomatoes, cilantro, chopped jalapeños, and black olives, gently mixing together

4. Finish by drizzling olive oil on the mixture, then cover and refrigerate.

5. Serve in small dishes or half-pint canning jars. Garnish with lime and the jalapeño slices.

MEDITERRANEAN ROASTED MACKEREL

PREP: 10 MINS   **COOK: 10 MINS**   **SERVES 2**

Mackerel is really low in calories and contains no carbohydrates. It's also a great source of calcium, vitamin D and B12.

INGREDIENTS

2 tablespoons olive oil

1 yellow onion, diced

2 cloves garlic, minced

1 800g can crushed tomatoes

½ cup olives, sliced

¼ cup capers

1 tablespoon paprika

1 teaspoon chili flakes

2 120g cans Mackerel

2 tablespoons lemon juice

Fresh chopped parsley for garnish

METHOD

1. Preheat oven to 350F. In a large skillet over medium-high heat, sauté the onions in olive oil until soft, about 3 minutes.

2. Add the garlic and cook for another minute. Add the canned tomatoes, olives, capers, paprika, and season with salt and pepper. Stir to combine and cook until heated through for about 3 minutes.

3. Meanwhile, in one large baking dish arrange the mackerel filets in an even layer. Pour the tomato mixture over the mackerel.

4. Roast in the oven for 8-10 minutes until the fish is cooked through. Remove from the oven and leave to rest.

5. To serve, sprinkle with chopped parsley and a squeeze of fresh lemon.

MEDITERRANEAN PENNE WITH ANCHOVIES AND TOMATOES

PREP: 10 MINS   **COOK: 10 MINS**   **SERVES 6**

INGREDIENTS

400g whole grain penne pasta

3 cups cherry or grape tomatoes, quartered

4 cups arugula, washed and trimmed

1 clove garlic, crushed

2 tablespoons extra-virgin olive oil

3 anchovy fillets preserved in oil, chopped OR 1/2 a teaspoon of anchovy paste

4 tablespoons grated Pecorino cheese (plus more for serving)

METHOD

1. Over high heat, bring a pot of salted water to the boil. Add the pasta and follow the cooking instruction on the packet. When tender, take a mug full of the salted pasta water and set aside. Drain the pasta.

2. Heat the olive oil in a saucepan over medium heat, and sauté the garlic and the anchovies for approx. 2 - 3 minutes.

3. Add the tomatoes combine with the oil. Cook for approx. 10 minutes and the sauce has thickened slightly.

4. Stir in the arugula until it wilts and season the sauce well with salt and pepper.

5. Add the cooked pasta and toss with the sauce. Add the pecorino. If you prefer your pasta sauce a little on the thinner side, stir in some of the reserved pasta water.

6. Serve in bowls with a drizzle of olive oil and more pecorino if desired.

MEDITERRANEAN COD

PREP: 2 MINS   **COOK**: 10 MINS   **SERVES** 4

This cod dish takes no time at all to put together; it's ready in a flash! Serve with salad and some crusty bread.

INGREDIENTS

4 cod fillets approx. ¼" inch thick

2 tablespoons olive oil

4 tomatoes, diced

¼ cup sliced black olives

1 pinch dried thyme

1 teaspoon dried basil

METHOD

1. Sprinkle cod with salt and pepper to taste.

Heat 1 tablespoon of olive oil in a large non-stick skillet over medium to high heat.

2. Add cod and cook for 30 seconds, turning once.

3. Toss the tomatoes and olives into the skillet with the cod and sprinkle over the thyme. Give the skillet a little shake to combine the ingredients and have them settle in a flat layer.

4. Reduce heat to low. Cover and cook 2 minutes. Add basil and drizzle the remaining olive oil. Cook covered for a further 1 to 2 minutes or until cod is opaque throughout.

MEDITERRANEAN STUFFED SWORDFISH

PREP: 15 MINS   **COOK: 20 MINS**   **SERVES 2**

INGREDIENTS

2 x 250g swordfish steaks (approx. 2" thick)

2 tablespoons olive oil

2 tablespoons fresh lemon juice

4 cups baby spinach

2 garlic cloves, crushed

1/3 cup feta, crumbled

METHOD

1. Preheat an outdoor grill or BBQ on high heat.

2. Cut a horizontal slit in each steak to create a small pocket, careful not to cut all the way through.

3. Combine 2 tablespoons olive oil and the lemon juice; using a pastry brush, generously oil both sides of the swordfish. Set aside.

4. In a small skillet, heat 1 teaspoon of olive oil and garlic over medium heat. Cook spinach until wilted, approx. 2 mins, and remove from heat. When cool enough to handle, push the spinach into the pockets. Also, place feta in the pocket on top of the spinach.

5. Place the fish on the grill, and cook for 8 minutes. Turn over, and continue cooking for another 6 minutes, or until cooked through.

SARDINE AND OLIVE TART

PREP: 5 MINS   **COOK**: 20 MINS   **SERVES** 4

This simple tart can be used for a light lunch, brunch or supper.
Serve with a salad or seasonal vegetables for a complete meal.

INGREDIENTS

1 sheet frozen puff pastry (thawed and halved)

125g canned sardines

1 ½ tablespoons oil

1 red onion, thinly sliced

12 black olives, pitted and halved

2 tablespoons flat-leaf parsley, finely chopped

METHOD

1. Preheat oven to 425°F. Line a baking sheet with baking paper. Place puff pastry on prepared tray. Lightly score a ½" border around edge of the pastry like a frame. Be careful not to cut all the way through.

2. Bake for 10 minutes or until lightly golden and puffed. Using a wooden spoon or spatula, press down the center of the pastry if it has fluffed up. Bake for 5 minutes more or until golden.

3. Heat reserved oil from sardines in a pan over moderately high heat. Add onion and cook, stirring, for 5 minutes or until onion softens and starts to brown. Season with salt and pepper.

4. Spoon onion mixture over the pastry. Half the sardines and arrange over onions. Sprinkle with olives. Bake for 8 minutes or until hot. Serve sprinkled with parsley.

BUCATINI ALLA PUTTANESCA

PREP: 10 MINS   **COOK**: 30 MINS   **SERVES** 4

INGREDIENTS

4 anchovy fillets, chopped

3 tablespoons olive oil

1 teaspoon finely chopped garlic

2 cups diced tomatoes

325g long pasta such as spaghetti or fettuccine

8 black olives, pitted and sliced

1 tablespoon capers, rinsed

1 teaspoon fresh oregano, roughly chopped

METHOD

1. Combine anchovies and 2 tablespoons oil in a large saucepan over medium heat. When the anchovies begin to dissolve, add garlic and stir for about 15 seconds. Add tomatoes and season well with salt and pepper.

2. Cook the tomatoes down until the sauce thickens, approx. 20 minutes. Remove from heat.

3. Bring a large pot of salted water to the boil. Add the pasta and stir to submerge all the pasta. Cook according to instructions on the packet until tender. Drain.

4. Return the sauce to medium heat. Add the olives, capers, and oregano; stir to combine.

5. Add the cooked pasta to the sauce and toss to combine. Serve immediately with a drizzle of olive oil.

MEDITERRANEAN SEARED SCALLOPS - ENTREE

PREP: 10 MINS   **COOK**: 10 MINS   **SERVES** 2

These scallops are the perfect start to any dinner party. Multiply the ingredients to suit your number of guests.

INGREDIENTS

6 scallops

1 tablespoon olive oil

50g halloumi cheese, cut in slices ¼" thick

50g cooked long pasta, spaghetti or fettuccine

1 large tomato

1 tablespoon coriander, chopped

½ red chili

¼ red onion, diced finely

1 tablespoon fig vinegar

2 dried figs

METHOD

1. Add all ingredients the chili, tomato, coriander, red onion, and dried figs to a food processor. Pulse to roughly chop all ingredients and create a salsa-like consistency.

2. Pat your scallops dry with kitchen paper. Halve each scallop horizontally to create 12 discs. Season with salt and pepper.

3. Add olive oil to a frying pan and wait until hot. Sear the scallops in the hot oil for about 1 minute each side. Transfer to a plate.

4. Sear the haloumi slices in the same pan as the scallops until golden brown on both sides.

5. To serve, divide the pasta between two plates in a nest shape. Place the scallops in the nest and top with the seared haloumi. Add the fig vinegar to the salsa and sear to combine. Add a spoonful to each plate, and serve.

GREEK BAKED SCALLOPS SANTORINI

PREP: 5 MINS   **COOK: 15 MINS**   **SERVES 2**

INGREDIENTS

450g scallops

1 teaspoon olive oil

½ cup onion, chopped

400g can diced tomatoes

1/4 cup dry white wine

3 cloves garlic, crushed

½ teaspoon dried oregano

2 tablespoons fresh lemon juice

50g feta cheese, crumbled

METHOD

1. Preheat oven to 450ºF. Rinse scallops and pat dry with a kitchen towel.

2. Cook onions in the olive oil over medium heat in a non-stick pan. Stir in tomatoes, wine, garlic, oregano, and lemon juice.

3. Reduce the liquid by half. Transfer the tomato mixture into a shallow casserole dish, and place scallops in and around the tomatoes.

4. Sprinkle with feta cheese. Bake for about 12 minutes or until scallops become opaque and firm.

5. Serve with pasta, rice, or cauliflower rice.

Chicken and Poultry

CHICKEN WITH SUNDRIED TOMATOES AND ARTICHOKES

PREP: 10 MINS   **COOK: 20 mins**   **SERVES 4**

Use gluten-free flour to coat the chicken to make this dish completely gluten-free.

INGREDIENTS

700g chicken breast, thinly sliced

¼ cup all-purpose flour

5 tablespoons olive oil

250g canned artichoke hearts, drained

200g sun-dried tomatoes

3 tablespoons capers, drained

2 tablespoons lemon juice

METHOD

1. Season the chicken breast strips with salt and pepper and coat with flour.

2. Heat 2 tablespoons of olive oil in a skillet over medium-high heat. Sear the chicken and transfer to a plate once golden brown on all sides.

3. Add the sun-dried tomatoes, artichokes, and capers with lemon juice to the same skillet. Add the remaining 3 tablespoons of olive oil. Stir to combine and heat through for 2 minutes.

4. Return the chicken to the pan and continue cooking for another 10 minutes or until the chicken is cooked through.

5. Serve with salad or Parmesan mashed potatoes.

GREEK CHICKEN WITH PASTA

PREP: 10 MINS   **COOK:** 30 MINS   **SERVES** 4

Save on the cleaning up with this quick and easy recipe, you'll only use one pan!

INGREDIENTS

½ cup Greek yogurt

2 tablespoons lemon juice

2 teaspoons fresh oregano, chopped

3 boneless, skinless chicken breasts, cut into chunks

1 teaspoon fresh oregano, finely chopped

350g penne pasta

3 cups chicken stock

1/2 cup black olives, sliced

1 cup cherry tomatoes, quartered

1 tablespoon lemon juice

½ cup feta, crumbled

1 tablespoon parsley, chopped coarsely

METHOD

1. Whisk together the Greek yogurt, 2 tablespoons of lemon juice and 2 teaspoons of oregano in a medium-sized mixing bowl. Add chicken and stir to coat. Refrigerate and allow to marinade for 15 minutes.

2. Heat large pan over medium heat. Add the uncooked pasta, chicken mixture, 1 teaspoon oregano and chicken stock. Season well with salt and pepper.

3. Bring to a boil and then reduce to a simmer. Cover and simmer for 15 minutes.

4. Remove from heat and stir in olives, tomatoes, lemon juice, and feta. Top with parsley and serve.

LEMON CHICKEN RISOTTO

PREP: 10 MINS   **COOK: 35 mins**   **SERVES 4**

Risotto is made with specific short grain rice called Arborio.

INGREDIENTS

500g chicken thighs cut into chunks

½ teaspoon garlic powder

½ teaspoon lemon pepper seasoning

2 tablespoons olive oil

1 tablespoon unsalted butter

1 1/2 cups Arborio rice

3 garlic cloves, crushed

1 cup dry white wine

5 cups chicken stock, warmed

1 teaspoon grated lemon zest

4 spring (green) onions, sliced into 1-inch long pieces

¼ cup grated Parmesan cheese

1 tablespoon fresh basil leaves, plus extra for garnish

1 tablespoon fresh parsley, plus extra for garnish

Lemon wedges for serving.

METHOD

1. Pat the chicken completely dry with paper towels. Season with the salt, garlic powder, and lemon pepper. Heat the oil in a large saucepan over medium heat. Once hot, add the chicken and cook in batches, transferring to a plate once cooked through.

2. Add the butter to the same pan. Add the rice and stirring continuously, toasting the rice until it's translucent, approx. 5 minutes.

3. Stir in the garlic and cook for another minute. Stir in the white wine, constantly stirring or at least stirring every minute or so, until the rice absorbs the wine. Once the wine is absorbed, add in 1 ½ cups of the warm stock, stirring continuously until the rice absorbs the liquid. Repeat this 2 to 3 more times; adding the stock in stages until all stock has been added and the rice is al dente. This process should take about 15 to 20 minutes. Aim to have a little liquid remaining at the end to serve.

4. Add in the onions, lemon zest, Parmesan, basil and parsley to the pan. Season with salt and pepper. Lastly, return the chicken to the pan.

5. Serve immediately with extra chopped herbs on top and lemon wedges on the side.

FENNEL CHICKEN PUTTANESCA

PREP: 10 MINS   **COOK**: 30 MINS   **SERVES** 4

INGREDIENTS

1 bulb fennel, sliced thinly

Olive oil

¼ cup Parmesan cheese

8 chicken thighs

800g can whole plum tomatoes

1 cup of green olives

1/4 cup capers

2 tablespoons garlic

2 tablespoons Italian seasoning

1/2 cup basil, roughly torn

METHOD

1. Preheat the oven to 400F. In a small baking dish, place fennel slices, olive oil, cheese, and garlic. Bake in the oven for 30 minutes.

2. Cook chicken thighs in a large pan with olive oil on medium heat. When the meat is cooked through and no longer pink, add in tomatoes. Using the back of a wooden spoon, break apart the tomatoes. Cook on medium for about five minutes.

3. Add in the green olives, garlic, capers, Italian seasoning, and basil. Reduce the heat to low and cook for another 15 minutes.

4. Add the roasted fennel to the chicken dish. Serve with a drizzle of olive oil.

PAN-ROASTED CHICKEN WITH OLIVES, FIGS, AND MINT

PREP: 20 MINS   **COOK:** 70mins + 4 HRS   **SERVES** 4-5

INGREDIENTS

1 whole chicken, approx. 1.6 kilo

1 tablespoon ground coriander

¼ teaspoon ground cinnamon

1/8 teaspoon cayenne

¼ cup olive oil

2 tablespoons roughly chopped pitted black olives

2 tablespoons roughly chopped green olives

8 dried figs, roughly chopped

1 tablespoon chopped mint, plus more for garnish

2 tablespoons fresh lemon juice

1 cup chicken stock

METHOD

1. Place the whole chicken on a cutting board, breast side down. Use kitchen shears to remove the backbone to

butterfly it and press the chicken with your hands to flatten it.

2. Stir together the salt, coriander, cinnamon, cayenne, and 2 tablespoons olive oil in a small bowl. Use your hands to rub the mixture all over the butterflied chicken. Skin side up, in the refrigerator uncovered for 4 to 24 hours.

3. Preheat the oven to 400F. Add the remaining 2 tablespoons olive oil to an ovenproof baking dish. Heat on high, and add chicken to the pan skin side down and cook until golden brown.

4. Transfer pan to the oven and cook for 30 minutes. Pour off any liquid that accumulates and turn the chicken over, skin side up. Add olives, figs, mint, lemon juice, and chicken stock to the pan and return to the oven for 30 minutes more.

5. When chicken is done, garnish with additional chopped mint. To serve, cut the chicken into quarters and drizzle each piece with pan drippings and olive and fig mixture.

EASY LEMON CHICKEN WITH ASPARAGUS

PREP: 10 MINS   **COOK**: 10MINS   **SERVES** 4

Add this simple dish to your family meal rotation for the nights you need to get dinner on the table in a hurry.

INGREDIENTS

500g boneless skinless chicken breasts

¼ cup flour

½ teaspoon salt, pepper to taste

2 tablespoons butter

1 teaspoon lemon pepper seasoning

1–2 cups chopped asparagus

2 lemons, sliced

2 tablespoons honey + 2 tablespoons butter

Parsley for garnish

METHOD

1. Cover the chicken breasts with plastic wrap and flatten out with a meat mallet until approx. ½" thick. Place the flour in a flat dish and season with salt and pepper. Toss each chicken breast in the dish, coating all over with the flour.

2. Melt the butter in a large frypan over medium-high heat. Add the chicken breasts and sauté for 3-5 minutes on each side, until golden brown. Sprinkle the lemon pepper on each side of the chicken as you go.

3. Remove from the pan and transfer to a plate once they are golden brown on both sides. Using the same pan, add the chopped asparagus. Sauté for a few minutes until the asparagus is bright green, and still crisp. Remove from the pan and set aside.

4. Lay the lemon slices flat on the bottom of the pan and cook for a few minutes on each side. Do not stir. You want the lemon to color and caramelize.

5. Remove the lemons from the pan and set aside. Layer all the ingredients back into the frypan – asparagus, chicken, and lemon slices on top and serve.

CILANTRO LIME CHICKEN WITH AVOCADO

PREP: 15 MINS   **COOK**: 12 MINS   **SERVES** 4

Chicken and avocado is a food match made in heaven. Add some cilantro and lime juice and I think you'll find this dish will be a family favorite.

INGREDIENTS

4 x boneless chicken breast

¼ cup lime juice

2 tablespoons olive oil

¼ cup fresh cilantro

½ teaspoon ground cumin

AVOCADO SALSA

4 small avocados, peeled and diced

½ cup fresh cilantro, diced

3 tablespoons lime juice

½ tablespoon red wine vinegar

½ teaspoon red pepper flakes

1 garlic clove, crushed

METHOD

1. In a ziplock bag, pour in the lime juice, olive oil, fresh cilantro, cumin and season with salt and pepper.

2. Add the chicken breasts to a zip lock bag making sure the chicken is well coated. Leave to marinade for 15 minutes. The lime juice will help to tenderize the chicken.

3. Heat an outdoor grill to medium heat or heat a large frypan on your stovetop to medium-high heat. Cook chicken for 4-7 minutes per side, or until cooked through. Allow chicken to rest in a warm spot while you make the salsa.

4. To make the salsa, combine all ingredients together in a small mixing bowl. Stir well to combine and season with salt and pepper.

5. Serve a chicken breast per person, and add a generous amount of salsa. This chicken would be lovely served with fresh corncobs, salad or rice.

HONEY-LIME CHICKEN PARCELS

PREP: 15 MINS   **COOK**: 12 MINS   **SERVES** 4

INGREDIENTS

3 tablespoons butter, melted

2 tablespoons olive oil

2 garlic cloves, crushed

1 tablespoon fresh ginger, grated finely

2 tablespoons honey

Zest of 1 lime

Four skinless chicken breasts

1 teaspoon cumin

½ teaspoon smoked paprika

1 bunch asparagus

2 ears corn, halved

2 tablespoons fresh cilantro, chopped

¼ cup thinly sliced green onion

METHOD

1. Add the butter, olive oil, garlic, ginger, honey and lime zest to a small mixing bowl and stir well to combine.

2. Using 12-inch sheets of foil, build four packets. Place a chicken breast in the center of each.

3. Divide the asparagus among the packets. Drizzle the chicken and asparagus with the honey-ginger sauce and season with salt and pepper. Fold the foil over the food inside and fold all the edges several times to ensure it's properly sealed.

4. Preheat a grill or grill pan over medium-high heat. Grill the packets until the chicken is cooked through, 10 to 12 minutes.

5. About 5 minutes before the chicken is finished, add the corn to the grill and cook until it's browned on all sides, about 5 minutes.

6. Sprinkle the chicken with cilantro and green onion to garnish before serving.

ONE-POT GREEK CHICKEN WITH ORZO

PREP: 5 MINS   **COOK**: 25 MINS   **SERVES** 4

INGREDIENTS

¼ cup olive oil

3 boneless chicken breasts cut into chunks

3 cloves garlic, crushed

2 tablespoon balsamic vinegar

1 tablespoon smoked paprika

½ cup fresh oregano chopped

2 bell peppers, sliced

1 cup of green olives

450g orzo pasta

150g feta cheese, crumbled

METHOD

1. Once hot, add the chicken, garlic, balsamic vinegar, smoked
   paprika, salt, and pepper. Toss the chicken to coat and then

cook until the chicken is browned all over and cooked through about 5 minutes. Stir in the oregano and cook another minute. Remove the chicken from the pan and to a plate.

2. To the same pan, add another tablespoon of olive oil, the bell peppers and a pinch of salt and pepper. Sear the peppers until just beginning to caramelize on the edges, about 3-4 minutes. Add the orzo and another tablespoon of olive oil. Stir the pasta with the peppers on then pour in 2 ½ cups water. Cook until almost all the water is absorbed and the orzo is creamy. If the orzo is not quite tender, add another ½ cup water and continue cooking. Stir frequently to avoid the orzo sticking to the pan.

3. Once the orzo is cooked, slide the chicken and olives into the orzo and remove from the heat. Allow the chicken to warm through, about 3 minutes.

4. Serve the dish topped with crumbled feta.

CHICKEN WITH COURGETTES

PREP: 10 MINS   **COOK:** 20 MINS   **SERVES** 4

This dish has some Asian inspired flavors that work beautifully with courgettes.

INGREDIENTS

1/3 cup soy sauce

1/3 cup rice vinegar

4 tablespoons sesame oil

700g boneless chicken thighs, cut into 3" pieces

1" fresh ginger, thinly sliced

3 cloves garlic, thinly sliced

1 teaspoon chili flakes

1 courgette, chopped

1 bell pepper, sliced

1 cup fresh basil

Rice for serving

METHOD

1. In a small bowl, combine the soy sauce, rice vinegar, and 2 tablespoons sesame oil.

2. Heat a large skillet over medium-high heat and add the remaining 2 tablespoons sesame oil. When the oil starts to shine, add the chicken and cook. Stir occasionally until the chicken is cooked through, approx. 8-10 minutes.

3. Add the ginger and garlic, and cook another minute more.

4. Pour in the soy sauce/rice vinegar mixture and toss in the courgettes and bell pepper. Cook until the sauce thickens slightly, about 6 minutes. Ensure all chicken and vegetables are coated well in the sauce.

5. Remove pan from the heat and stir in the fresh basil. Serve with steamed rice.

ITALIAN TURKEY MEATBALLS

PREP: 20 MINS   **COOK:** 20 MINS   **SERVES** 4

Turkey is very lean and very tasty. However, this recipe will work with any ground meat, such as chicken, beef or lamb.

INGREDIENTS – MEATBALLS

1 pound lean ground turkey

1/2 medium onion grated
3 garlic cloves minced
1/4 cup minced flat-leaf parsley
1/4 cup whole wheat breadcrumbs
1 egg
1 teaspoon ground oregano

INGREDIENTS – SAUCE

2 teaspoons olive oil
1 small onion, diced
3 garlic cloves, crushed
1 teaspoon ground oregano
¼ teaspoon chili flakes
1 800g can crushed tomatoes
1 400g can crushed tomatoes
1/4 cup minced flat-leaf parsley
4 basil leaves, sliced

METHOD – MEATBALLS

1. Preheat the oven to 350 degrees F. Lightly coat a baking sheet with cooking spray.

2. In a large bowl, stir together the ground turkey, onion, garlic, parsley, breadcrumbs, egg, oregano, salt, and pepper.

3. Divide the mixture into 8 portions, form into balls and place on the prepared baking sheet.
4. Bake until the meatballs are firm to the touch and cooked through approx. 15 to 20 minutes.

METHOD – SAUCE

1. Heat the olive oil in a large non-stick skillet set over medium heat. Add the onion and cook until softened, about 5 minutes.
2. Stir in the garlic, oregano, salt, and pepper, and cook for 1 minute.
3. Add the crushed tomatoes, bring the sauce to a boil, and then simmer for 10 minutes. Stir in the parsley and basil.
4. Nestle the meatballs into the sauce and spoon sauce over to coat the meatballs.
5. Serve over pasta or rice, or on its own.

This sauce and the meatballs freeze very well. Make large batches and freeze in airtight containers for a quick midweek meal.

WHOLE ROASTED ROSEMARY SPATCHCOCK

PREP: 20 MINS   **COOK:** 20 MINS   **SERVES** 6

The term "spatchcock" refers to how the chicken has been cut. Spatchcock chickens have been split open and butterflied, leaving the bones in. This allows the chicken to cook much quicker and it looks impressive when served.

INGREDIENTS

2 whole spatchcock chickens

3 tablespoons fresh rosemary, chopped

4 tablespoons butter, softened

1 lemon, zested

METHOD

To spatchcock the chickens, place it breast side down with the legs facing toward you. Using kitchen scissors or shears, cut along each side of the backbone and remove it. Using the flat side of a knife, break the wishbone. Turn the chicken over, breast side up. Use the palm of your hand and push the chicken down to make it lay flat.

Using a sharp knife, make small slits at the joint between the drumstick and the thigh; and also the joint between the wing and the breast.

1. Light charcoal grill or preheat oven to 425F

2. Season the chickens on both sides with salt and pepper, and brush with the softened butter. Sprinkle with rosemary.

3. Place the chicken on the grill with the legs closest to the flames; however make sure the chickens are not over direct flames. Close the lid of the grill and roast the chicken for 30-40 minutes, until cooked through.

4. Let the chickens rest for about 5-10 minutes covered with foil. Serve the spitchcock chickens cutting into pieces

Red Meat

MORROCAN BEEF TAGINE

PREP: 15 MINS   **COOK**: 1 HRS 45 MINS   **SERVES** 4

INGREDIENTS

800 g Gravy Beef cut into bite-sized chunks

1 large onion, diced

6 garlic cloves, finely diced

1 Large butternut squash, cut into bite-sized chunks

1 400g can of chickpeas, rinsed and drained

1 400g canned tomatoes

1 Tablespoon tomato puree

100g prunes

1 liter vegetable stock

1 Tablespoon olive oil

3 Tablespoons Moroccan Spice

1 tablespoon cumin

1 tablespoon Cinnamon

1 tablespoon Ground Ginger

1 tablespoon coriander

1 tablespoon Paprika

Red Chili Pepper (optional)

METHOD

1. In a small bowl add all the seasonings/spices and mix well to combine. Rub the seasoning/spices into the beef. Toss well ensuring the spices are evenly distributed over the beef. Cover and refrigerate for an hour.

2. Place the garlic and onion in the tagine with the olive oil and cook over medium heat for 2 minutes or until the

onion softens. Add the beef and fry for a further 5 minutes or until the beef is sealed all over.

3. In a blender, combine together the tinned tomatoes, vegetable stock, prunes, tomato puree, and drained chickpeas. Add them to your tagine. Bring it to the boil and once it has come to the boil, reduce the heat and simmer for 15 minutes.

4. Add the butternut squash to the tagine and give everything a stir, add the lid and cook for a further 90 minutes on medium-low heat.

5. Add chili flakes if you like a little spice. Serve with warm crusty bread.

If you find the stew is drying out, add a little extra vegetable stock. If you don't have a traditional tagine, you can use a flameproof casserole dish or a Dutch oven.

MEDITERRANEAN BRAISED BEEF

PREP: 15 MINS   COOK: 2 HRS 30 MINS   SERVES 6-8

Slow cooking is made for lazy Sunday afternoons with family. Share a bottle of red wine, and this succulent pot roast.

INGREDIENTS

1 boneless beef chuck shoulder pot roast, 1 – 1.3kg

¼ cup all-purpose flour

2 tablespoons olive oil

¼ cup balsamic vinegar

2 small onions, halved, sliced

4 medium shallots/spring onions, sliced

¼ cup chopped pitted dates

METHOD

1. Heat oven to 325°F. Lightly coat beef with flour, and season with salt and pepper all over. Heat oil in a Dutch oven over medium heat. When hot, brown the pot roast on all sides; remove.

2. Add 1-1/2 cups water and vinegar to Dutch oven; cook and stir until brown bits attached to pan are dissolved.

Return pot roast. Add onions, shallots, dates, salt, and pepper; bring to a boil.

3. Cover tightly and cook in 325°F oven 2 to 2-1/2 hours or until pot roast is fork-tender. Remove pot roast; keep warm.

4. Cook liquid and vegetables over medium-high heat to desired consistency. Carve pot roast. Serve with sauce and garnish with fresh parsley if desired.

GREEK BEEF IN TOMATO SAUCE

PREP: 5 MINS   **COOK:** 60 MINS   **SERVES** 6

INGREDIENTS

1.3 kg stewing beef, cut into cubes
1 large onion, diced
1 tablespoon granulated sugar
3 garlic cloves, crushed
1 bay leaf
1 large cinnamon stick
¼ teaspoon ground cloves

400g can diced tomatoes

4 tablespoons tomato paste

3 tablespoons olive oil

½ cup beef stock

½ cup red wine

2 tablespoons flat leaf parsley, chopped coarsely

METHOD

1. Heat a tablespoon of olive oil in a large cast-iron casserole dish or Dutch oven, over high heat. Brown the beef, in batches, until nicely colored on all sides. Remove, transfer to a plate. Repeat with the remaining beef, adding more olive oil if required.

2. Heat another tablespoon of olive oil in the same pan and lower the heat to medium. Add the onion and sugar, cook over medium heat for about five minutes, until softened.

3. Add the garlic, bay leaf, cloves, salt, pepper, and cinnamon stick and stir for a couple of minutes until fragrant.

4. Stir in the chopped tomatoes, tomato paste, beef stock, and red wine. Add the beef, stir together and cover.

5. Turn the heat down to a low simmer, and cook the beef for 45 minutes, stirring occasionally.

6. Stir in the chopped parsley. Serve with mashed potatoes, rice or orzo pasta.

GARLIC & ANCHOVY ROASTED LAMB CHOPS

PREP: 10 MINS   **COOK:** 25 MINS   **SERVES** 2-3

INGREDIENTS

3 garlic cloves, crushed

2 anchovy fillets, chopped very finely

1 teaspoon anchovy oil

½ teaspoon cracked black pepper

6 lamb chops, room temperature

2 tablespoons olive oil

¼ cup unsalted butter

10 olives, pitted and chopped

8 fresh sage leaves

METHOD

1. Preheat oven to 375°F. Place garlic, anchovies, anchovy oil, and black pepper in a small bowl and whisk together. Lightly season lamb chops with salt and pepper. Brush garlic-anchovy mixture over each chop, on both sides.

2. Pour olive oil into a large sauté pan and place over medium-high heat. Sear each chop in the pan for 2 to 3 minutes, on each side, and transfer to a roasting pan.

3. Roast lamb chops for about 13 to 15 minutes for medium-rare, and 15 to 18 minutes for medium. Remove from the oven and allow chops to rest for 5 minutes.

4. Using the same pan you used to sear the chops, melt the butter over medium-low heat. Allow butter to cook for 6 to 8 minutes or until the butter has melted and begins to foam and brown. Add olives and sage leaves and gently fry for 1 to 2 minutes. Remove mixture from the heat. Season with salt and pepper.

5. Transfer chops onto a serving dish/platter and pours butter sauce over chops. Serve immediately.

MOROCCAN GOAT CURRY WITH MAKFOUL

PREP: 20 MINS   COOK: 4 HOURS   SERVES 4-6

INGREDIENTS – CURRY

2 tablespoons coconut oil
1 – 1.3kg whole goat shoulder
1 onion, chopped
2 cloves garlic, chopped
1 teaspoon salt plus more to taste
1 teaspoon turmeric
1 teaspoon ground cumin
1/2 teaspoon ground ginger
1/2 teaspoon ground coriander
1/2 teaspoon ground fenugreek
1/2 teaspoon cayenne pepper
1/2 teaspoon black pepper
1/4 teaspoon ground cloves
1 pinch (10 strands) saffron

2 cups chicken stock
3 bay leaves
3 green cardamom pods
1 cinnamon stick

INGREDIENTS - MAKFOUL

1 tablespoon olive oil
1 onion, thinly sliced
4 tomatoes, chopped
1 pinch salt
1 tablespoon honey
¼ fresh parsley, chopped

This curry is traditionally made in a tagine. If you don't have a tagine, a large flameproof casserole dish will suffice.

If you are unable to obtain goat meat, this curry will also work very well with lamb shoulder. The slow cooking process of this Moroccan curry achieves tender results with both goat and lamb.

METHOD – GOAT CURRY AND MAKFOUL

1. Heat the oil in a tagine or Dutch oven over medium-high heat. Brown the shoulder on both sides, about 3 minutes per side.

2. Set the shoulder aside, reduce the heat to medium and add the chopped onion. Sauté until softened, about 4 minutes. Add the garlic, ground seasonings and saffron. Sauté until aromatic, about 30 seconds, then stir in the chicken stock and add the bay leaves, cardamom, and cinnamon.

3. Return the goat to the pot, bone side down; bring to a simmer, then cover and reduce the heat to low. Simmer for 2 hours, then flip the goat over and simmer for 1 more hour.

4. To make the Makfoul, heat olive oil in a pan and add the sliced onion. Sauté until softened, about 3 minutes. Add the chopped tomatoes and a pinch of salt. Continue to sauté the onion and tomato until caramelized, about 45 minutes, stirring every 5 minutes. Once caramelized, stir in the honey and reduce the heat to low to stay warm.

5. When the goat is tender and easily pulls away from the bone, remove it from the tagine and set it on a cutting board to rest for 10 minutes. As the shoulder rests, remove the bay leaves, cardamom pods, and cinnamon stick from the tagine.

6. Increase the heat to medium and gently reduce the liquid by 1/3 to concentrate the flavors. Return the heat to low. Once the goat has rested, remove the bones and cut up the meat into bite-sized pieces.

7. Return the goat meat to the tagine, season with salt and pepper. Serve in bowls with rice, flatbread and a spoonful of Makfoul atop the curry. Garnish with chopped parsley.

MEDITERRANEAN LAMB BOWLS

PREP: 15 MINS   **COOK:** 20 MINS   **SERVES** 4

INGREDIENTS

450g ground lamb

1 tablespoon olive oil

¼ cup finely diced onion

4 cloves garlic, crushed

1 teaspoon paprika

1 teaspoon allspice

1/2 teaspoon red pepper flakes

1/4 teaspoon ground ginger

1/4 cup fresh mint, chopped plus more for garnish

1/4 cup flat leaf parsley, chopped plus more for garnish

For Bowls

1 cup Turmeric Rice or other rice of choice

1 tomato diced

1 cucumber peeled and diced

1 cup hummus homemade or store-bought

1 cup feta cheese

2 pita bread optional, for serving

METHOD

1. Heat a large sauté pan over medium heat and add the olive oil.

2. Once the oil has heated, add onions and garlic and sauté for 5 minutes.

3. Add ground lamb. Brown lamb until cooked through.

4. Add paprika, allspice, red pepper flakes, ginger, salt, and pepper. Stir until fully combined and evenly distributed. Cook for 1-2 minutes. Remove from heat and stir in fresh herbs.

5. In a bowl, layer rice, then top with some of the spiced ground lamb, tomatoes, cucumbers, hummus, and feta. Sprinkle with more fresh mint and parsley if desired.

MIDDLE EASTERN MEATBALLS IN SAFFRON CURRY SAUCE

PREP: 20 MINS   **COOK:** 30 MINS   **SERVES** 4

INGREDIENTS - MEATBALLS

2 ½ cups fresh rustic bread - cubed

680g ground lamb

450g ground beef

2 eggs

8 cloves garlic, crushed

1 tablespoon sweet paprika

2 teaspoons ground ginger

1 ½ teaspoon ground turmeric

1 teaspoon cumin

¼ teaspoon ground cinnamon

¼ teaspoon ground cloves

½ teaspoon ground coriander

¼ cup fresh Italian parsley, finely chopped

¼ cup cilantro, finely chopped

¼ cup green onions, finely chopped

METHOD – MEATBALLS

1. Preheat oven to 350 degrees F. Scatter the chopped bread onto a baking sheet and toast for approximately 10-15 minutes or until the bread is dry and no longer moist and soft. When finished toasting, remove the bread from the oven and transfer to a large mixing bowl.

2. Allow the bread to cool for approximately 5 minutes before adding the milk. Mix well until the toasted bread is fully coated and all milk has been absorbed.

3. To the same mixing bowl add the lamb, beef, eggs, garlic, spices, and fresh chopped herbs. Using your hands, mix well to thoroughly combine the meat, bread, and spices.

4. Increase oven heat to 375 degrees F. Line two large baking sheets with baking paper. With damp hands, roll the meat mixture into approximately 1.5" sized meatballs.

5. Transfer each meatball to the prepared baking sheet, repeating the process with all the meat mixture. Transfer baking sheets to preheated oven and bake for approximately 20 minutes. Remove from oven.

INGREDIENTS – SAFFRON CURRY SAUCE

1 tablespoon olive oil

1 large yellow onion - diced

8 cloves garlic - minced

¼ teaspoons ground cumin

400g canned crushed tomatoes

125g tomato paste

1 pinch saffron

2 cinnamon sticks

1 ½ cups chicken stock

2 tablespoon honey

½ cup chopped walnuts

½ cup golden raisins

1 ½ cups milk

METHOD – SAFFRON CURRY SAUCE

1. Heat olive oil in a saucepan or Dutch oven over medium-high heat. Add the onion to the pot and sauté until soft and translucent, approx. 5 minutes.

2. Add the garlic, cumin, salt, and pepper to the onions and mix well to combine. Cook for an additional minute, stirring continuously.

3. Add the crushed tomatoes to the onions and mix well. Allow tomato juices to come to a low boil before adding the tomato paste. Mix well to combine.

4. Remove the onion and tomato mixture from the heat allow to cool slightly. Use a stick blender to process the mixture completely smooth.

5. Add the saffron, cinnamon sticks, chicken broth, and honey to the sauce and mix well to combine. Cover and simmer for approximately 10 minutes, stirring occasionally.

6. Remove the cinnamon sticks from the sauce and stir in the milk mixing well to combine. Add the chopped walnuts and golden raisins, if desired.

7. Return sauce to a low simmer before adding the pre-cooked curried lamb meatballs to the pot.

8. Allow the meatballs and sauce to simmer for 5 minutes before garnishing with additional chopped fresh parsley. Serve with warm couscous or rice.

MEDITERRANEAN BEEF STEW

PREP: 10 MINS   **COOK**: 1 HR 45 MINS   **SERVES** 6

A warm beef stew on a winter's night is the ultimate comfort food. Serve with mash potatoes or pasta and crusty bread.

INGREDIENTS

1/4 cup vegetable oil

1.3kg beef chuck roast, cut into bite-sized cubes

2 onions, chopped

3 celery stalks, diced

4 cloves garlic, minced

2 800g cans Italian-style stewed tomatoes

1 cup dry red wine

1/2 cup chopped fresh parsley

1 teaspoon dried oregano

METHOD

1. In a soup pot over medium-high heat, heat oil until hot; brown beef on all sides.

2. Add onions, celery, and garlic, and sauté 5 minutes or until vegetables are tender. Add remaining ingredients and bring to a boil.

3. Reduce heat to low, cover, and simmer 1 and ½ hours to 1 and ¾ hours or until beef is fork-tender.

GRILLED BEEF SHAWARMA

PREP: 20 MINS   **COOK**: 8 MINS   **SERVES** 6

This Beef Shawarma is a great dish to share with friends, set everything out on platters and let everyone help themselves!

INGREDIENTS – SPICE RUB

1 teaspoon ground cumin

1 teaspoon ground coriander

1 teaspoon sweet paprika

3/4 teaspoon ground turmeric

1/2 teaspoon ground cloves

1/2 teaspoon cayenne pepper

1/2 teaspoon ground cinnamon

INGREDIENTS - SHAWARMA

800g beef flank steak (about 1/2 inch in thickness)

Olive oil

3 garlic cloves, crushed

INGREDIENTS TO SERVE

4 Pita pockets halved

Arugula and/or fresh parsley

1 to 2 tomatoes, sliced

Pickles

1 red or yellow onion, sliced

Tahini Sauce and/or Hummus

METHOD

1. In a small bowl, mix together the shawarma spices. Set aside for now.

2. Season the steak on both sides with salt and pepper. Brush both sides olive oil, then spread the minced garlic on each side.

3. Rub each side of steak with a generous amount of the shawarma spices. Let the steak rest at room temperature for 30 minutes before cooking.

4. While the steak is resting, get the pita and fixings. Arrange on a platter ready to serve.

5. Heat a grill on high. Give the steak another brush of olive oil. Grill on high heat for 3 to 4 minutes per side, turning over once. This will give a medium rare result. Cook for longer if you prefer your meat cooked further.

6. Transfer steak to a cutting board and let rest for 5 to 7 minutes. Cut against the grain into thin slices.

7. Serve grilled beef shawarma in pita pockets with the fixings you've prepared on your platter.

SPANISH PAPRIKA BEEF

PREP: 40 MINS   **COOK**: 1 HOUR   **SERVES** 8

This is a classic Spanish dish that is sure to please the fussiest of eaters.

INGREDIENTS

2 kg gravy beef, cut in large rustic pieces

¼ cup olive oil

1 large red capsicum, deseeded and roughly chopped

2 large onions, chopped roughly

4 carrots, peeled and chopped

1 400g can crushed tomatoes

4 garlic cloves, crushed

4 bay leaves

2 teaspoons fresh thyme, chopped or 1 teaspoon dried thyme.

3 tablespoons of Spanish sweet paprika

2 cups of dry white wine

3 cups low salt beef stock

½ cup green pepper stuffed olives

METHOD

1. Preheat the oven to 180°C. Using a heavy bottomed deep sauté pan or casserole, add half the olive oil and brown the beef all over then remove from the pan.

2. Pour the white wine into the sauté pan and stir it to deglaze all the delicious browned beef flavor from the pan, then reserve.

3. Dry the pan with kitchen roll. Pour the remaining olive oil to the pan. Add the onion and cook gently until softened and lightly browned, add the garlic and stir until it starts to smell fragrant, add tomatoes, capsicum, carrots,

herbs, paprika, stock and return the meat and wine to the casserole, season to taste.

4. Increase the heat to high and cook for about 20 minutes until the sauce starts to thicken slightly. Then transfer to bake in the oven (about 2 hours) until the meat is tender and the sauce is reduced. Add the olives in the last 10 minutes of cooking.

5. Sprinkle with parsley and serve piping hot straight from the oven with steamed rice and vegetables.

ITALIAN BEEF RAGOUT

PREP: 15 MINS   **COOK**: 2.5 HOUR   **SERVES** 4

INGREDIENTS

2 tablespoons olive oil

750g gravy beef, trimmed, cut into 3cm cubes

1 large brown onion, finely chopped

2 garlic cloves, crushed

2 medium carrots, peeled, halved, sliced

2 celery stalks, sliced

4 slices pancetta, chopped

2 tablespoons plain flour

2 dried bay leaves

2 sprigs fresh thyme

2 sprigs fresh rosemary

2 tablespoons chopped fresh sage leaves

2 tablespoons balsamic vinegar

1 cup red wine

1 cup beef stock

400g can diced tomatoes

Cooked pasta, to serve

METHOD

1. Preheat oven to 180°C/160°C fan-forced. Heat half the oil in a large, heavy-based, flameproof casserole dish over medium-high heat. Cook beef, in batches, for 5 to 6 minutes or until browned. Transfer to a bowl.

2. Heat remaining oil in the dish. Add onion, garlic, carrot, celery, and pancetta. Cook, stirring, for 5 minutes or until onion has softened. Return beef to the dish. Add flour. Cook, stirring, for 1 minute. Add bay leaves, thyme, rosemary, and sage.

3. Stir in vinegar, wine, stock, and tomato. Cover. Bring to the boil. Transfer to oven. Bake for 2 hours or until beef is tender. Serve with pasta.

MEDITERRANEAN LAMB PIZZA

PREP: 5 MINS   **COOK**: 20 MINS   **SERVES** 4

Traditional take away food gets a makeover with this healthy burger option.

INGREDIENTS

Olive oil

1 large red capsicum, quartered, deseeded

3 large courgettes, peeled into thin ribbons

1 (about 150g) lamb fillet

4 small rounds pita bread

2 tablespoons basil pesto

50g feta crumbled

80g low-fat ricotta, crumbled

1 tablespoon toasted pine nuts

Fresh basil leaves, to serve

METHOD

1. Preheat oven to 200°C. Preheat grill on high. Spray a large baking tray with olive oil spray to lightly grease. Place the capsicum, skin-side up, on the prepared tray. Lightly spray with olive oil spray. Cook under the grill for 5 minutes or until charred and blistered. Transfer the capsicum to a sealable plastic bag and set aside for 5 minutes (this helps lift the skin). Peel the skin from the capsicum and cut the flesh into thin strips.

2. Drizzle a little olive oil into a frying pan. Heat over high heat. Add the zucchini and cook, stirring, for 3-4 minutes or until the courgette is tender. Transfer to a heatproof bowl. Season both sides of the lamb with salt and pepper. Add to the pan and cook for 2-3 minutes each

side for medium or until browned. Transfer to a plate and cover with foil. Set aside for 3 minutes to rest. Thinly slice the lamb across the grain.

3. Spread the bread with pesto. Sprinkle with the cheese. Top with the courgette, capsicum, lamb, and ricotta.

4. Place the pita bread on 2 baking trays. Bake in the oven for 10 minutes or until the cheese melts and the base is crisp. Sprinkle with pine nuts and basil leaves to serve.

LAMB ROAST WITH LEMON AND WHITE WINE

PREP: 15 MINS   **COOK**: 3.5 HOURS   **SERVES** 4

Traditional take away food gets a makeover with this healthy burger option.

INGREDIENTS

1 tablespoon olive oil

1.8kg lamb shoulder roast (bone in)

2 onions, peeled, sliced

4 sprigs rosemary

375ml chicken stock

125ml white wine

6 anchovies, finely chopped

2 tablespoons capers, rinsed, drained

1 lemon, juiced

4 garlic cloves, crushed

1 lemon, extra, thinly sliced

1 cup drained olives

2 x 400g can cannellini beans, rinsed and drained

1/2 cup cream

2 tablespoons lemon juice, extra

METHOD

1. Preheat the oven to 150°C. Heat half the oil in a large frying pan over high heat. Season the lamb. Cook for 5 mins or until browned all over. Transfer to a plate.

2. Place the onion, in a single layer, in the base of a large roasting pan. Top with 2 sprigs of rosemary and then the lamb. Make slashes in the top of the lamb. Place 1 cup (250ml) of the stock in a jug. Stir in the wine, anchovies, capers, lemon juice, and half the garlic. Season. Pour over the lamb. Top lamb with lemon slices and remaining rosemary sprigs. Cover the pan tightly with foil and roast for 3 1/2 hours or until lamb shreds easily with a fork, adding the olives in the last 30 mins of cooking.

3. Meanwhile, heat the remaining oil in a frying pan over medium heat. Add the remaining garlic and cook for 1 minute. Add the beans, cream and remaining stock. Cook for 10 mins or until mixture thickens slightly. Stir in the extra lemon juice. Using a stick blender, blend the beans until smooth. Season.

4. Shred the lamb and serve with white bean puree and seasonal vegetables. Spoon over the sauce.

MEDITERRANEAN MEATLOAF

PREP: 5 MINS   **COOK**: 3.5 HOURS   **SERVES** 4

INGREDIENTS

1/2 cup brown rice

1 small red onion, grated

350g lean beef mince

1 carrot, peeled, grated

60g low-fat feta cheese, crumbled

2 tablespoons tomato sauce

1 egg, lightly beaten

2 tablespoons basil leaves, shredded

1 courgette, thinly sliced

375g cherry tomatoes

1 garlic clove, crushed

Olive oil cooking

METHOD

1. Cook rice following absorption method on the packet. Set aside to cool.

2. Preheat oven to 200°C. Grease base and sides of a 7cm-deep, 10cm x 18cm (base) loaf pan. Line with baking paper, allowing a 2cm overhang at both long ends.

3. Combine rice, onion, mince, carrot, feta, sauces, egg and basil in a bowl. Mix well. Press into prepared pan.

4. Place courgette, tomatoes, and garlic in a bowl. Spray with oil. Toss to combine. Spoon over meatloaf. Bake for 60 to 80 minutes or until meatloaf is firm. Stand for 10 minutes. Slice and serve.

VEAL CAMPAGNOLA

PREP: 10 MINS   **COOK**: 7 MINS   **SERVES** 4

Veal is the meat from calves. It's known for being incredibly lean and tender.

INGREDIENTS

1/2 cup plain flour

1 tablespoon ground paprika

4 veal steaks

30g butter

1 tablespoon olive oil

3 slices tomato

375g jar passata sauce

125g mozzarella cheese, sliced

Fresh basil leaves

Salad, to serve

METHOD

1. In a shallow dish mix together the flour, ground paprika
   and season with salt and pepper. Dust 4 veal or steaks in
   flour mixture, coat well and shake off any excess.

2. Heat butter and 1 tablespoon olive oil together in a large
   frying pan on high heat. Cook meat for 1 minute each
   side. Arrange a single layer in a shallow ovenproof
   casserole dish.

3. Preheat a grill to high. Top each piece of meat with a slice of fresh tomato and drizzle passata tomato sauce over. Top with mozzarella. Grill for 4-5 minutes until melted and golden brown.

4. Finish by sprinkling with fresh basil leaves. Serve with a fresh salad or steamed greens.

VEAL SCALLOPINI WITH SPICY TOMATO SAUCE AND CAPERS

PREP: 5 MINS   **COOK**: 20 MINS   **SERVES** 4

INGREDIENTS

Olive oil

4 (125g each) veal schnitzels

1 small red onion, finely chopped

1 garlic clove, crushed

1/4 teaspoon dried red chili flakes

1/4 cup white wine

400g canned diced tomatoes

1 tablespoon salted baby capers, rinsed, drained, finely chopped

2 teaspoons balsamic vinegar

1/4 cup fresh basil leaves

METHOD

1. Heat a large non-stick frying pan over high heat. Add a drizzle of olive oil and cook the veal for 1-2 minutes each side for medium-well or until cooked to your liking. Transfer to a plate and cover with foil to keep warm.

2. Reduce the heat to medium. Add the onion and cook, stirring occasionally, for 3-4 minutes or until soft. Add the garlic and chili and cook, continually stirring, for another minute. Add the wine and simmer until reduced by half.

Add the tomato and capers and simmer for 5-10 minutes or until the sauce thickens slightly. Stir in the vinegar.

3. Add the veal and turn to coat in the sauce. Top with the basil leaves and serve with baby potatoes and rocket.

MEDITERRANEAN STUFFED PORK CUTLETS

PREP: 15 MINS   **COOK**: 20 MINS   **SERVES** 4

INGREDIENTS

2 chat potatoes

1 tablespoon extra virgin olive oil

4 x 200g pork cutlets, trimmed

1/3 cup finely chopped semi-dried tomatoes

2 tablespoons grated Parmesan

2 tablespoons pine nuts, toasted

1/3 cup basil pesto

80g baby spinach

1 tablespoon balsamic vinegar

METHOD

1. Pierce potatoes all over with a fork. Place on a plate and cover with a paper towel. Microwave 3 to 4 minutes or until just tender. Using a potato masher, or the flat side of a knife, gently press each potato to squash slightly. Place in a medium bowl with olive oil and toss to coat.

2. Use a sharp knife to cut a horizontal slit into the side of each pork cutlet to make a pocket. Combine tomatoes, Parmesan, half the pine nuts and 1 tablespoon of basil

pesto in a small bowl. Stuff tomato mixture into each pocket.

3. Heat a greased barbecue hotplate or grill on medium heat. Cook pork for 5 to 7 minutes on each side or until just cooked through. Cook potatoes on a barbecue with pork for 2 to 3 minutes each side or until browned and crisp.

4. Serve with chargrilled vegetables or salad.

SPICY LEMON AND GARLIC PORK

PREP: 15 MINS   **COOK**: 10 MINS   **SERVES** 4

INGREDIENTS

2 tablespoons lemon juice

2 garlic cloves, crushed

1 teaspoon cracked black pepper

2 teaspoons ground paprika

1/4 teaspoon cayenne pepper

1 tablespoon olive oil

4 Pork Cutlets

1/2 cup flat-leaf parsley, chopped

50g feta, crumbled

METHOD

1. Mix lemon juice, garlic, pepper, paprika, cayenne pepper and olive oil in a medium bowl. Add pork and turn to coat, season with salt and pepper and stir to combine.

2. Heat a large frying pan over medium-high heat. Cook pork for 3 mins each side or until browned and cooked through. Transfer to a plate, cover with foil and allow the pork to rest for 5 minutes.

3. Transfer the cutlets to service plates and crumble over the feta cheese and parsley. Serve with fresh garden salad and lemon wedges.

MEDITERRANEAN LAMB AND VEGETABLE COUSCOUS

PREP: 15 MINS   **COOK**: 45 MINS   **SERVES** 4

INGREDIENTS

2 green courgettes, ends trimmed, coarsely chopped

4 aubergines, ends trimmed, coarsely chopped

1 red bell pepper, halved, deseeded, thinly sliced

1 red onion, halved, cut into thick wedges

4 garlic cloves, unpeeled

Olive oil spray

2 vine-ripened tomatoes cut into wedges

150g couscous

185ml boiling water

500g lamb backstraps

1/3 cup loosely packed torn fresh basil

20g baby rocket leaves

1 tablespoon fresh lemon juice

1 tablespoon white wine vinegar

2 teaspoons olive oil

METHOD

1. Preheat oven to 180C. Combine the courgettes, aubergines, bell pepper, onion and garlic in a large baking dish. Lightly spray with olive oil spray. Bake in preheated oven for 20 minutes or until just tender.

2. Add the tomato to the courgette mixture and bake for a further 15 minutes or until tomato softens slightly. Remove from oven. Transfer garlic cloves to a small bowl and set aside.

3. Place the couscous in a large heatproof bowl and pour over the boiling water while stirring with a fork. Cover and set aside for 10 minutes or until all the liquid is absorbed. Use a fork to separate the grains.

4. Preheat a barbecue or chargrill on high. Season the lamb with salt and pepper. Cook lamb on preheated grill for 3 minutes each side for medium-rare or until cooked to your liking. Transfer to a plate and cover with foil. Set aside for 5 minutes to rest. Thickly slice the lamb across the grain.

5. Add the zucchini mixture, lamb, basil and rocket to the couscous and gently toss until just combined.

6. Squeeze the garlic flesh into a small bowl. Add the lemon juice, vinegar and oil, and use a fork to whisk until well combined. Taste and season with salt and pepper. Drizzle the salad with dressing and gently toss until just combined. Spoon salad among serving plates and serve immediately.

Confess! abot
ovoid.
escapesn:
Epheo 4: 32
Rom. 12:19
Matt 5: 44
Matt. 11: 28-30

CPSIA information can be obtained
at www.ICGtesting.com
Printed in the USA
BVHW030153170320
575220BV00001B/121